Pastoral Spirituality

Pastoral Spirituality
A Focus for Ministry

Ben Campbell Johnson

W
P

The Westminster Press
Philadelphia

Unless otherwise identified, scripture quotations are from the Revised Standard Version of the Bible, copyrighted 1946, 1952, © 1971, 1973 by the Division of Christian Education of the National Council of the Churches of Christ in the U.S.A., and are used by permission.

The quotation marked TEV in Guided Reflection 6 is from *Good News Bible: The Bible in Today's English Version.* Old Testament: © American Bible Society, 1976; New Testament: © American Bible Society, 1966, 1971, 1976.

The excerpts from *Amadeus* by Peter Shaffer in chapter 3 are copyright © 1980, 1981 by Peter Shaffer. Reprinted by permission of Harper & Row, Publishers, Inc.

First edition

Published by The Westminster Press®
Philadelphia, Pennsylvania

PRINTED IN THE UNITED STATES OF AMERICA
9 8 7 6 5 4 3 2 1

Library of Congress Cataloging-in-Publication Data

Johnson, Ben Campbell.
  Pastoral spirituality : a focus for ministry / Ben Campbell
Johnson. — 1st ed.
      p.   cm.
  Bibliography: p.
  ISBN 0-664-25003-3 (pbk.)
  1. Clergy—Religious life. 2. Clergy—Office. I. Title.
BV4011.6.J64 1988
248.8'92—dc19   88-10050
                                                        CIP

Contents

Preface

One of the most critical issues facing the church today is that of pastoral identity. Who am I? Who am I in Christ? Who am I in the role of minister of Christ? The search for authentic identity requires ministers to discover their own spiritual depths and relate them to the functions of ministry.

For at least a generation the minister has been caught in a false professionalism, one that imitates secular counterparts instead of forging an appropriate profession: that is, defining the work of one who has been called by God. The consequence of this diversion has sometimes been the creation of clergy who are entertainers in the pulpit, managers of religious organizations, consultants to spiritual practitioners, therapists for the hurting, ambitious career seekers. This perversion of the ministry cannot save a church from irrelevance or its members from meaninglessness.

I am convinced that the call of God offers the focus for a recovery of pastoral identity and an appropriate pastoral spirituality that can inform the practice of ministry. Nothing short of a conviction that one's life has been claimed by God can serve as the foundation for the servanthood for which clergy men and women have been called.

I have had two audiences in mind. First, I have written for men and women who are beginning their ministry. The foundation for ministry is spiritual, the call of God in Christ; and this call shapes the vision of the practice of ministry. Second, I have written for ministers who have been in the parish for a dozen or so years. For many the struggle for survival, the impoverishment of their souls, and the scars of battle have dulled the sense of call and the vision of Christ in the simple, concrete acts of ministry.

Pastoral Spirituality addresses two foci of ministerial identity: the being of the minister and the doing of ministry. The being of the minister stems from the individual minister's relation to God by creation, call, and consecration. This being, which is the foundation of the minister's spirituality, develops in a matrix that includes time, community, context, and destiny.

Spiritual awareness grows through a deepened self-awareness through time with the support of appropriate disciplines.

The doing of ministry begins with one's being; the minister ministers by *being* a minister of God. Doing ministry also includes the structuring of time through the liturgy and the celebrations of the Christian year and serving as a sacramental presence at the passages of life. Ministry expresses itself in guiding persons on their personal journey and in shaping the ministry of the church to re-present Christ to the world. The hallmark of ministry is expressed in servanthood. Servanthood is not a distinct category but a style that pervades all of the ministry practiced by the man and the woman called by God.

The Appendix of this book contains Guided Reflections to aid you in relating the themes of the respective chapters to your own experience in ministry. A series of exercises, one for each day in a week, is suggested for each chapter. Whether the reflections are actually done on consecutive days does not matter; what matters is that they are done. The Appendix also contains a brief introduction to journal writing. Keeping a journal of your thoughts and reflections will aid you in becoming more aware of God's calling to you in your experience.

In many ways this book is about me more than you. It defines my own struggles to be an authentic disciple who has been called to minister. The hard sayings of this book are directed first to me and then to you, in a secondary sense. Yet I hope you and I both will be given a new sense of call—a deeper vision of what ministry entails—and that through this gift both we and the church of Jesus Christ will be quickened.

I am debtor to many persons. First, to the Master of Divinity students in my spring 1987 class at Columbia Theological Seminary who used the outline of this book as a text and offered numerous suggestions for revision. A special thanks to Scott Ellington, who did some additional research for me. The members of a doctoral class I conducted in Jefferson City, Tennessee, added their voices. I am also indebted to a number of colleagues who have read the text and made important suggestions for its revision.

Special thanks to Nan, my wife and secretary, who typed the original draft and sacrificed time with me so that I could finger the computer in the production of this text.

1 The Minister of God

Late Saturday evening at the end of a busy week, the minister struggled in his book-lined study, trying to pull together a sermon for the Sabbath.

The phone rang.

"Hello?"

"With whom am I speaking?"

"Thomas MacGreggor. The Rev. Thomas Louis MacGreggor."

"Am I interrupting your work?"

"No, I have time to talk."

"I haven't heard from you in several years, and I wondered how things are going with you."

The voice sounded familiar, but Tom did not immediately identify the person making this warm inquiry. "I don't believe I caught your name. Who did you say this is?"

"Tom, this is Jesse Van Meeter. I've just moved to Edenton in response to a call from the United Church."

"Jesse! What a terrific surprise!" Hearing the name reminded Tom of the close relationship he had shared with this friend and mentor. Jesse's home had been a haven for Tom during his seminary years. The older man had counseled him in times of stress and ministered to him at critical junctures in his life. For Tom, Jesse O. Van Meeter was as close to being the voice of God as anyone he knew.

Tom hadn't heard from Jesse since seminary graduation. He had, however, received Jesse's Christmas letters signaling his continued interest.

"How have things been going with you?"

How many times through seminary had he heard that question from Jesse! Just like old times. Jesse was one of those people you might not see for years, but his first word made you feel you had seen him yesterday. Tom's reverie was interrupted when Jesse repeated his question.

"How have things been going with you?"

"OK, I suppose. My family feels a little neglected. And sometimes I feel confused. You know, I left a secure job in real estate to go to work for God. I graduated from seminary with stars in my eyes, but now I find the work of a minister much like any other job—only it's religious."

Jesse responded sympathetically, his tone reassuring. He communicated the genuine interest in Thomas MacGreggor that he had always shown. "What have you been doing this week?"

"What have I been doing . . . ?" The words trailed off as Tom began recounting the events of the week:

Visited the hospital daily to check on Mrs. Smythe, who has been in the process of dying for weeks; spoke with Jim Hayes, a leader in the church, who just found out that he has cancer; talked to Mark Jones about a major gift to the building program; counseled the Baxters and the Hansons about their marriages; spent half the day Wednesday trying to convince the women of the church to provide a meal for the stewardship campaign; caught the devil from Bill Longley for inept administration (a career employee of IBM, Bill thinks the church ought to be run like a corporation); and, besides these demands, the usual number of committee meetings, emergency phone calls, and kids' soccer games. . . .

Tom's review was interrupted by Jesse's next words.

"Is it still fun?"

The blunt question forced Tom to admit to himself that, no, it wasn't still fun. It had been fun once. He had a fleeting glimpse of the vision he took with him to seminary. He had been called by God. He remembered his eagerness to get out of seminary and serve God. He would participate with God in a ministry to the world! What excitement!

They talked a while longer, and then Jesse offered a parting word: "Whatever is going on in your life, don't forget who called you. God did not call you to forsake you." With that admonition, Jesse invited Tom to visit him in Edenton and said goodbye.

The study was quiet again. The open commentaries were still spread over the cluttered desk; ideas for tomorrow's sermon came as awkwardly as before. Tom's mind was whirling from the conversation. Why had Jesse called? He had not been in Tom's life for several years. Why now?

Unable to get back into the sermon for a moment, Tom let memories from seminary days and the first few years in the parish come flooding over him. Guiltily, he acknowledged that the haunting images from earlier days had been grossly betrayed by a business-as-usual, task-oriented approach, as shown by the routine of the past week.

How compelling his vision had been when he left his real estate business to go to seminary! He had felt himself truly called by God for the work of ministry.

In those days he pictured himself sent by God to a congregation he would serve as the minister of Christ. He had frequently envisioned himself leading a faithful, enthusiastic congregation in the worship and service of God.

Ah! This would be a vibrant community shaped by the events of Christ's life and regularly punctuated by celebrations of the events of the Christian year.

Although he knew little about what one of his professors described as "the inner way," he had had a longing to walk with people through the deep places of their lives.

He remembered the pastoral leadership course, which gave him a vision of committees as the organized, functioning body of Christ; these work groups were Christ taking physical form in a particular time and place. What a contrast to the dull, pointless committee meetings he had attended this past week.

Tom also recollected that when he decided to leave the real estate business, Margie, his wife, had asked some sharp and insightful questions. What would it mean to their two children, then five and seven? What would be her new role as a minister's wife? How would their lives change?

Tom came to himself; he awoke as from a dream to find that the sermon had not written itself while he was away in fantasy land. But the vision lingered. Perhaps, after all, God could speak through him in the morning! With renewed zeal he set about writing the sermon for the next day.

Isn't there a part of Tom in all us preachers? Was his first vision of ministry an illusion? What happens to us? Is there any help for the flatness of spirit even the busiest pastor may feel? Can we recapture even for a moment that primal vision of ministry? Perhaps we must begin where Tom began, with that singularly most important fact that *we have been called by God.* The call of God creates the core of a minister's life and spirituality. Perhaps a review of the call of God will throw light both on Tom's dilemma and on our own.

The Call of God

All ministers at some level believe themselves to be called by God. The experience of a "call" originates with the caller, who speaks out to another. The act takes the form of an utterance, summons, signal, or formal invitation. For the call to be effective, it must be heard. It may come as startling, gentle, sudden, gradual, or demanding. To hear a call orients one's life; the reorientation becomes a vocation or profession.

The Bible describes the call as coming before we were: that is, in a suprahistorical setting; it began in the mind and heart of God. Actually, the divine call originated in the election of God "before the foundation of the world" (Eph. 1:4). God chose us, the whole fallen race, in Jesus Christ before the world was created. Call has its theological fountainhead in this gracious love of God bestowed upon us before we were anything but a thought in the mind of God.

What then does it mean for a man or a woman to be called by God? A call presupposes that God has foreknown and elected that person to a relation with godself; it means God has made this call known in Jesus Christ. Professor Karl Barth says:

> The Word of the living Jesus Christ is the creative call by which He awakens man [sic] to an active knowledge of the truth and thus receives him into the new standing of the Christian, namely, into a particular fellowship with Himself, thrusting him as His afflicted but well-equipped witness into the service of His prophetic work.[1]

This affirmation of the call of God suggests two questions relevant to our inquiry: What is the relation of the general call to all persons to God's special call to ministers? And how does a minister's call relate to a minister's spirituality?

In answer to the first question, we recognize that all persons are called to faith in Jesus Christ; all are called to a vocation of witness in the world. In this sense all are ministers; all are God's priests. But Christ has given special gifts to the church, gifts of leadership (Eph. 4:11–13). These gifts or offices include apostles, prophets, evangelists, pastors, and teachers. The persons who fill these offices "equip the saints for the work of ministry" (v. 12). These offices focus the task of the ordained ministry on the members, who must be prepared for their world-oriented witness.

Paul claims a call to his apostolic office. In the introduction to two letters he states: "Paul, a servant of Jesus Christ, called to be an apostle, set apart for the gospel of God" (Rom. 1:1) and "Paul, called by the will of God to be an apostle of Christ Jesus, and our brother Sosthenes" (1 Cor. 1:1). His credentials depend on being "called to be an apostle."

But Paul points out that not all are called to these offices. To correct the confusion in the Corinthian church, he states: "And God has appointed in the church first apostles, second prophets, third teachers, then workers of miracles, then healers, helpers, administrators, speakers in various kinds of tongues" (1 Cor. 12:28). Having made this clear declaration of God's appointment, he asks a series of rhetorical questions: "Are all apostles? Are all prophets? Are all teachers? Do all work miracles? Do all possess gifts of healing? Do all speak with tongues? Do all interpret?" (vs. 29–30). The expected answer to these questions is evident.

We conclude, therefore, that all are called to Christ and are united in his body, but not all have the same calling within the body. Paul claims he was "called to be an apostle"; certain persons are called to offices of ministry within the church. Paul was called to be an apostle; other persons are called to be prophet, evangelist, pastor, or teacher. This line of reasoning justifies the minister's special call to an office in the church. This special call must not, however, be seen as distinct from the call to faith. Rather, it is continuous with the initial call. The call to an office is an extension, a clarification, a focusing of the initial call. Neither does this special call elevate the minister over the laity.

The laity, too, are called to a vocation of witness to Christ. These witnesses are also servants of Christ, but their primary ministry takes shape in the world. The pastor or teacher, as a servant of Christ, equips the members of the body of Christ for their ministry of witness wherever they have been scattered in society.

Having related the minister's call to the general call to faith, we now inquire how the call relates to the minister's spirituality. Spirituality originates in the call of God. As a person becomes aware of the interventions of God in life and responds to those invitations to faith and love, the result is a deepening awareness of God. Awareness of the call of God and responsiveness to this call stand at the heart of pastoral spirituality. God's continuous call provides the dynamic element in spirituality, and our response forms it. The office also provides the minister certain formal aspects of his or her spirituality; preaching, teaching, and leading are examples. We will concern ourselves now with how the call and the formal aspects of the office shape the minister's spirituality and how the various offices are enriched and fulfilled through that spirituality.

Tom MacGreggor had heard the call of God. Perhaps God had called him before his birth, an aspect of call that was at best a matter of faith. Whatever the background, he had felt confronted by Christ at a lay retreat he attended in his late twenties; he could not shake the conviction that he had to prepare for ordination. His experience after that retreat was like being awakened from a deep sleep, like finding a marked pathway when he was lost in a maze. After he surrendered himself to what he understood as God's will, he had felt at peace with himself. He recalled coming home from the office, sitting down with Margie, and telling her that for the first time in his life he was truly happy.

But now Tom's feelings were just the opposite. Often he was tired; his work was never finished; he had settled into a business-as-usual style of ministry. The call from Jesse shocked him into admitting that it *wasn't* fun anymore. What could he do? How could he have a compelling vision for his life and ministry? How could he hear the call anew? Perhaps to remember God's earlier call would sensitize him to God's call today.

Special Call

As we have seen, the minister receives a particular call from Christ to express his or her obedience in an office of the church—a special function. All persons are called by the Spirit into the community of Christ; this is the meaning of Christ's universal call to all persons who were chosen in him before the foundation of the world. All persons called into a relation with Christ are also called to witness (Acts 1:8). All believers must be equipped to participate in the witness of Christ to the world (Eph. 4:8–12). For new creatures participating in the body of Christ and ministering in the world, there is no distinction between the ordained minister and the lay person. The essential distinction involves place and role: the ordained minister in the church, the lay person in the world.

After the telephone call from his old friend that Saturday night, Tom began in earnest to reconsider his role as a minister. Was he truly called? Had he deluded himself in a moment of sudden emotion? Glancing over at the bookcase, he saw a small book with a yellow cover protruding from the others as if asking to be picked up and read. He reached for it. *The Purpose of the Church and Its Ministry* by H. Richard Niebuhr had been an important book for him while working through his call years ago. Perhaps it could help him again.

According to Niebuhr, all persons are called to be Christian.[2] There is no distinction between the minister and the lay person with respect to this call to personal faith. Those who are called to ministry have previously been called to personal faith in Christ.

This call may come in a variety of ways. For some, faith is the result of the Spirit's activity through nurturing families, loving Sunday school teachers, and faithful Christian witnesses. For others, the call to faith is more dramatic. They may be marginal church members or outside the church when they are confronted with the gospel of Christ. This confrontation and their response in faith result in a changed life.

The call to faith does not predispose one toward ministry. But the initial call to faith provides the context within which a person hears the call to a particular office within the church.

Providence endows some persons with the gifts, the temperament, and the capacity for ministry. These persons have high ideals, love people, and hope to make a difference in the world. One study indicates that ministers often come from homes in which the father is away and the mother is the primary caregiver. They grow up with a sense of responsibility for the world. During adolescence they often do not fit in with their peers. In high school they serve as hall monitors or editors of school papers; they are more identified with the adult world than with that of their peers.[3]

The providential aspect of a call traces the handiwork of God in the events of one's life. On reflection a person discerns impressions, open doors, the response of friends, and a thousand "funny little things" that confirm the call of God. This reflection results in a conviction that God has destined one for ordained ministry.

Niebuhr defines the secret call as an inner persuasion of the Spirit that one has been called by God. The process of that inner secret call begins with an idea that persists; it attracts interest. The individual responds by envisioning life as a minister. This awareness generally initiates a struggle followed by an affirmation of the call. The person whom God calls often tests this secret call by practice runs at ministry; for example, serving as the liturgist at worship or teaching a Sunday school class. Following such acts of ministry, members of the congregation may sense the Spirit's work and suggest that the individual would make a good minister.

Sometimes the secret call is more dramatic. The Spirit through the Word of God, the witness of a believer, or a providential act may reveal to a person the call of God. When this occurs, the person has a deep, unavoidable sense of being grasped by God for a purpose.

A call is also issued by the church. The institutional call includes a recommendation from the governing body of a congregation. In all churches the call of a person to ministry must be approved by the community of faith. The particular form of recognition depends upon the polity of the denomination. In a congregational form, ordination depends wholly upon the congregation; in presbyterian polity, ordination comes through the session, the congregation, and presbytery; in the episcopal form, congregations and vestries recommend and concur but final power resides in the bishop.

Acceptance by a theological seminary constitutes an aspect of the church's testing of the call. The church has a long history of discerning the call of Christ in its members. When the providential call, the secret call, and the natural call converge, the church takes on the responsibility of supporting a person on the journey toward ordination.

The call of God constitutes the fountainhead for the minister's spirituality. This call creates a man or woman of God. When filled with the Spirit, Christ manifests himself in this called person. Yves Congar has described the character of this person: "The virtue of God rests on him [sic], animates him, acts through him and often goes beyond the limits of what is ordinary because of a discernment of spirits, a power over souls, prophetic lights and the gifts of knowledge."[4]

What on this earth can hold greater significance than the conviction that the Eternal Mystery knows a person's name, elects that person for a role in the divine mission to the world, discloses that call in human consciousness, and confirms it by nature, inner persuasion, providence, and the polity of a particular church? This call of God defines the center and the parameters of each pastor's spirituality, but the subjective experience of call is not permanent.

The insistent and irrepressible nature of this call came home to Tom at a ministerial meeting shortly after the Saturday evening phone call. The devotional was given by the Episcopal rector, who indicated that a book on spirituality had challenged him regarding his personal call. He read from the introduction:

" 'God's call is mysterious; it comes in the darkness of faith. It is so fine, so subtle, that it is only with the deepest silence within us that we can hear it. And yet nothing is so decisive and overpowering . . . on this earth, nothing surer or stronger. This call is uninterrupted: God is always calling us! But there are distinctive moments in this call of his, moments which leave a permanent mark on us—moments which we never forget.' "[5]

The quotation so impressed Tom that he asked for a copy. As he reflected on those words describing God's call, they underscored the continuous nature of the call of God. God had been calling him for a long time; God was calling him now; God would continue to call in the future.

Loss of the Sense of Call

While the call of God provides the impetus for the minister's spiritual development, the awareness of the call sometimes fades from consciousness; the call loses its convictional quality. In the press of conflicting responsibilities, the minister can easily forget who he or she is called to be. When the minister loses this sense of call and special role in the body of Christ, ministry becomes diffused, and ministerial burnout comes close behind. The minister becomes a hollow person with no clear sense of identity, spiritual power, or conviction and little relish for the daily tasks of ministry.

In his discussion of vocation, Barth recognized the need for the renewal of the call. He stressed that the "personal calling as such stands in need of constant repetition and renewal, and therefore never stands so fully behind [the person] that it is not also before."[6] This renewal represented a need of Tom's, but how to hear the call anew?

Tom MacGreggor had always tried to be honest with himself; the crisis in his identity drove him to seek counsel from his trusted friend, Jesse Van Meeter. He sat in the old minister's study. The room was dim; books were spread across the desk; a worktable in the corner was stacked with papers, correspondence, and a "must" list of reading material. Yet there was a reassuring air of confidence in the room.

Tom began with his most pressing question. "What happens to a minister when the sense of call grows dull?"

Jesse leaned back in his chair, closed his eyes, and thought for a long time. When he spoke, his words struck fear in Tom's troubled soul.

"When you lose the sense of call," he said, "you become a religious functionary without spiritual depth. In this bland state you carry out the functions of your role without a sense of the holy."

Expanding his answer, he drew word pictures of different identities of the minister who has become estranged from this transcendent call. "Without a sense of call, the minister becomes an administrator of a branch office of the institution . . . or a public relations director for a religious corporation . . . or a psychologist with a neutral morality assisting persons in their personal and social adjustment . . . or an ethicist who aims to restructure society in harmony with an idealization of the kingdom of God . . . or a philosopher of religion who dispassionately examines ideas about God and the world . . . or a church employee who seeks to make a contribution to the world while having a 'successful' career . . . or an ecclesiastical politician who seeks to direct the denominational powers but is often distracted by the operations of the bureaucratic machine.

"When the minister falls prey to one or more of these bastardized roles, about all that is left is retirement. Unable to change vocations, the minister waits for the day of release." He paused, a look of sorrow on his face.

Pastoral Stagnation

As Tom prepared to leave his friend's study, the senior pastor reached between the covers of an old Bible and pulled out a yellow sheet that showed the wear of years.

"Here's a list of symptoms I pay attention to. Through the years, when I have recognized them in my life, I have changed my priorities."

Tom took the sheet, made a copy, and sent the original back to his spiritual mentor. In the quiet of his study he began checking his own symptoms against the list.

1. Activity increases, filling consciousness with trivial tasks but leaving little awareness of God.

2. Tiredness prevails; every action requires more and more effort.

3. There are feelings of disorientation and loss of clear direction.

4. Joy in ministry is lost; duty prevails.

5. Life and ministry seem ambiguous; nothing feels right.

6. The future seems lost, bleak and hopeless, which causes depression.

7. Preaching has a dullness akin to prerecording and continues from habit, with little sense of the presence and reality of God.

8. Encounters with holy things do not stir the soul.

9. Doubts are everpresent: of one's self, of one's competency, of the faith, and sometimes of God.

10. God recedes from consciousness and seems unreal, distant, or absent.

11. Prayer is sparse, professional, or nonexistent.

12. Preaching becomes increasingly abstract, deals with issues without reference to faith, and seems belabored and dull.

13. Conversation about personal faith and the experience of God is avoided.

These symptoms follow when the man or woman called by God loses touch with God's call. The wise minister must surely guard against the catastrophe that follows these harbingers. But suppose it does happen? Tom MacGreggor found himself manifesting too many of these symptoms for his own comfort. The counsel of his trusted minister friend deepened his conviction that changes had to be made in his priorities. What was he to do? How was he to reconcile his feelings of separation with the minister he longed to be?

Loss of Call as Invitation

The existential loss of call, as bleak and painful as it may be, is an invitation. The experience of alienation from one's spiritual depth, from the call of God, leaves a person feeling helpless. In anguish the soul cries out, "I can't deliver myself; I can't go on as a phony; I can't make it unless something happens to me!" In an effort to endure, ministers sometimes sink into a paralysis of inactivity.

An alternative to avoidance of the pain is to face it, to turn intentionally into the emptiness, to embrace one's own void, and to listen for God in the silence of one's soul. "It is only with the deepest silence within us that we can hear it," Carlo Carretto says.[7] The Spirit has not abandoned the life of a tired, confused, and overwhelmed minister. The Presence may have been stifled, but the Presence has not been extinguished. The Spirit does not issue a call with the intention of forsaking the minister of God, whether that minister is young or old. Do not fear the darkness; the darkness beckons us into intimacy with our Lord.

The pain of emptiness invites the minister to stop, to notice, to listen to God. Have you ever seen a row of trees with a strand of barbed wire attached? As the trees grow, they have strange ways of responding to the presence of the wire. Some resist it, and the resistance produces scars and stunted growth. Others absorb the wire without the least evidence of struggle. These trees take the wire right into their heart. Perhaps we, too, need to open ourselves to the pain of our emptiness and let it instruct, even penetrate our heart. If we open ourselves to it, it will become a part of us.

To resist leaves only the option of running away from the pain. How productive will this be?

Security of the Call

Whatever our experience may be of disillusionment, shallowness, or burnout, the call of God stands secure. Even when our experience and performance are ambiguous, unfaithful, and seemingly ineffective, God still calls us. Any minister who has followed Christ for a time has passed through the valley of shadows; that minister knows the sense of utter futility, which wipes out vision and saps energy, leaving little hope for the future. How can any minister who has been so wounded call this darkness an invitation from God?

This emptiness of soul should be looked upon as an invitation from God for three reasons. First, the decision of God to call is an irrevocable, unshakable decision by the Holy One. The covenanting God is "for us." Our performance, or the lack of it, does not change God's decision about us.

God not only calls with an irrevocable call; God loves us, an equally strong reason to look upon our darkness as an invitation. This emptiness expresses a call from God because of God's unchanging love. Remember Paul's admonition:

> Who shall separate us from the love of Christ? Shall tribulation, or distress, or persecution, or famine, or nakedness, or peril, or sword? . . . No, in all these things we are more than conquerors through him who loved us. For I am sure that neither death, nor life, nor angels, nor principalities, nor things present, nor things to come, nor powers, nor height, nor depth, nor anything else in all creation, will be able to separate us from the love of God in Christ Jesus our Lord.
>
> Romans 8:35, 37–39

Does not the apostle indicate that our darkness can be a call when he says:

> We know that in everything God works for good with those who love him, who are called according to his purpose. For those whom he foreknew he also predestined to be conformed to the image of his Son, in order that he might be the first-born among many brethren. And those whom he predestined he also called; and those whom he called he also justified; and those whom he justified he also glorified.
>
> Romans 8:28–30

God works through every circumstance of our lives to make the call unmistakable.

Our darkness can be the occasion of God's invitation because a certain maturity only comes in the darkness. The Christmas cactus does not bloom until it is first hidden in the dark; the darkness invites the plant to produce its beauty. Ministers' lives are like that. Some with great gifts for preaching and giving of ministry seem green or immature because they lack the maturity that darkness invites. The darkness cannot offer us its transformative power if we run away from it.

About three weeks after his first visit with Jesse, Tom had a word of assurance that he believed was from God. On this particular morning Tom had risen early for a time of silence. He was pondering the question of his call: Can I continue in the ministry? Is there any way out of my emptiness? By a quirk of fate or by the providence of God, his reading was from the eleventh chapter of Romans. When his eyes fell on verse 29—*"For the gifts and the call of God are irrevocable"*—it read like a telegram from God. This declaration gave him the courage to face into his darkness, to embrace the uncertainty of the future, and to go forward with God in obedience and hope.

A persuasion of call that will not let go sustains the spirituality of the pastor.

2 The Matrix of Pastoral Spirituality

After a couple of weeks, Tom went for another visit with his old friend. Reflecting on the danger signals his mentor had given him had left Tom feeling guilty and confused.

"I need something more," he heard himself confessing.

"This 'something more,' what is it?" Jesse asked.

"I'm not sure, but it must have something to do with God and me," Tom answered.

"I'd call it spirituality," Jesse said firmly.

"Spirituality? The very word makes me cringe," Tom retorted.

"Looks like there's something behind that reaction, something that pushed your button," the older man responded with a chuckle.

Tom knew exactly what created his disgust. "It was in my first parish that the word went sour for me. . . . Are you sure you want to hear this story?" he added.

"Sure. Go ahead," came the reply.

"In my first church I had an elder named Jim Councilman. He was a nominal churchman when I arrived on the scene, and I spent some time with him. Both he and I were seeking to deepen our relation with God. In a few months, as they say, 'He got religion.' I noted that he seemed to be in a race to prove he was more spiritual than I was.

"One day Jim came to me with a look of concern on his face. 'How much time are you spending in prayer, Tom?' he asked with a note of urgency.

" 'Not much this week; I've been terribly busy,' I said.

" 'I thought so,' Jim responded. 'I can tell it in your preaching.'

"Jesse, he got so caught up in his spirituality that he fasted for thirty consecutive days, eating nothing but bread and water, and all the time he worked at a job that was physically demanding.

"After that experience, he met me in the sanctuary one Sunday morning with this greeting, 'Tom, God has given me the sermon; the Lord spoke to me this morning in my prayer time and told me I was to preach today.'

"Quickly, with more than a trace of anger, I told him, 'Well, I was speaking with the Lord myself and God didn't mention it to me!' Jim was put off by my words, and from that time our relationship deteriorated."

"So that's what lies behind your hostile reaction," Jesse said.

"That's only part of it. After a particular meeting of the church officers he accosted me about mentioning the Vietnam war and the injustices we foster in the Third World. He declared that if I stuck to preaching the gospel and left those social issues alone, the church would be better off and people's souls would be fed."

"And you let this misguided soul intimidate you," Jesse said reprovingly.

"No, I don't think Jim intimidated me; he disgusted me to the point that I wanted nothing to do with him or with spirituality if his attitude was the product of a spiritual quest.

"I suppose the last straw came when he resigned from the board," Tom continued. "He handed me his resignation with this parting shot: 'Preacher, I just can't take the shallow spiritual life of this church anymore. I'm leaving. You pointed me to the Word. Now, I've got Jesus and the Word and that's all I need.' "

"So," Jesse said, "you're letting the unfortunate experience of one man's perverted spirituality turn you away from the source of reality and power."

"I wouldn't have chosen those words, but I suppose that's what I have done," Tom admitted.

Jesse slipped into preaching. "When you begin exploring the meaning of spirituality, you'll meet some folks who make the Bible a literal word of God and claim they possess the infallible interpretation; others will hide an inflated ego behind their spiritual certainty; some will make their spirituality private, forsaking the institutional church and isolating their faith from the issues of the day—"

"OK, OK," Tom interrupted. "I get the message. Where do I begin?"

His spiritual guide puffed on his pipe, blew a ring of blue, scented smoke toward the ceiling, and looked steadily into Tom's eyes for a few moments. Then he leaned back in his chair, closed his eyes, and told this story.

"Once upon a time there was a small village which had only one rabbi. The rabbi was old and lived alone. He had a donkey, upon which he rode.

"One day he was seen riding his donkey along one of the village streets. 'Where are you going, rabbi?' shouted the children.

" 'I'm looking for my donkey,' he called back.

"He was a servant of God riding a donkey looking for his donkey."[1]

Tom understood. He was sitting astride the "stuff" that offered him both the starting point and the substance of his spirituality.

To help the Tom MacGreggors and Jim Councilmans, the church needs a larger vision of spirituality and its formative elements. We are, therefore, addressing the question of the meaning of spirituality and its substance in the life of the minister of God. In condensed form here is a suggested answer: *The spirituality of the pastor flows from a relationship with God, mediated and formed in a community of faith, expressed in the world in a limited period of time as the minister seeks to fulfill her or his destiny. These different elements—God, self, church, time, community, and destiny—form the matrix within which, from which, and into which spirituality is formed.* (Figure 1 illustrates these six elements in the matrix.)

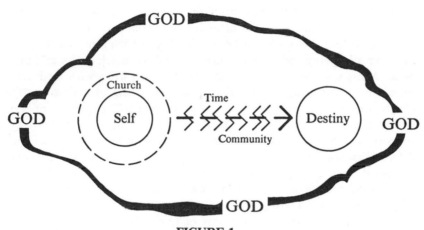

FIGURE 1.
A matrix for spirituality.

Originally, the word "matrix" referred to a womb; later, it designated a female animal that was kept for breeding purposes. By implication, matrix came to mean "that by which, within which, and from which something takes form or develops." A matrix in this context typifies the personal, spiritual, temporal, social, and teleological structure in which spirituality is conceived, gestated, born, and sustained.

The matrix of pastoral spirituality may be compared to wrestlers in a ring, in an arena in a particular section of town. Despite the fake displays seen on television today, the wrestling analogy for spiritual development has biblical warrant (Gen. 32:22–32). Paul uses athletic imagery frequently, and it is one of the singularly most important motifs in his writing. One scholar says that "in Paul's letters the moral struggle is not infrequently pictured in the form of an athletic contest," an image that emphasizes the idea of progress, growth of character, and strenuous moral exertion.[2]

According to Paul we "run the race, keep the body in subjection, and contend for the faith." He also speaks of wrestling "not against flesh and blood, but against principalities, against powers, against the rulers of the darkness of this world, against spiritual wickedness in high places" (Eph. 6:12, KJV).

The minister is a wrestler with evil. The minister also wrestles with God, and the wrestling match provides an apt image for spiritual growth. The match takes place in a limited time and space signified by the ropes around the ring. And the struggle occurs in the midst of eager, excited onlookers who sometimes encourage and support the wrestler and at other times shout angrily and throw things into the ring. The meaning of each encounter is retained in the memory of the wrestler as his future unfolds in the various bouts of his career. The arena itself sits in a larger community; it has a mailing address designating its place in the outside world.

The minister develops his or her spirituality in such a matrix. It is a lot like a wrestling ring with its boundaries, onlookers, participants, and opponents. Many ministers spend considerable time wrestling with God; sometimes they must struggle with themselves and their own destiny. (One glaring weakness of this analogy must be addressed. The minister does not wrestle the forces of evil alone. The congregation enters into the struggle, supports and encourages the minister, and shares in both the victories and defeats. Perhaps a tag team for the wrestling match enlarges the metaphor, making it more appropriate.) The components of this matrix, this area of struggle and new birth, will make more sense when we have defined spirituality, the fruit of the struggle.

One of the best generic definitions of spirituality has been offered by Urban Holmes:

> I am defining spirituality as (1) a human capacity for relationship (2) with that which transcends sense phenomena; this relationship (3) is perceived by the subject as an expanded or heightened consciousness independent of the subject's efforts, (4) given substance in the historical setting, and (5) exhibits itself in creative action in the world.[3]

An examination and critique of the elements in this definition will give shape to the spiritual matrix. An addition of the elements of church, time, and destiny will round out other dimensions that should also be included.

Human Capacity for Spiritual Awareness

According to Holmes's definition, spirituality begins with a "human capacity for relationship." To have a relationship, one must have a self, an I who encounters a Thou. This encounter is possible only when one has an identity. Human beings created in the image of God have the capacity to be aware of themselves as separate from other selves and the power to create an identity, a distinct narrative that holds meaning for them.

Spirituality as a human capacity includes being aware, naming, interpreting, remembering, connecting, narrating, anticipating, and editing. Reflect on these capacities as they relate to spirituality.

Each person has an awareness: that is, a capacity to notice and identify what is taking place, either in the outer world of things or the inner world of intuition and imagination.

The ability to name that awareness, intuition, or feeling lifts it out of the flux of stimuli and shapes it into a definite experience. The naming of the act or experience consists of assigning a symbol to it. Without a name the experience cannot be analyzed for its content and message to the life of an individual.

The person who has this experience also has the capacity to interpret the meaning of it for his or her life. The experience may be good or bad, joyous or painful, beneficial or hurtful; or it may carry very little meaning at the time. Nevertheless, the person interprets life experience, and the interpretation of experience provides life with definable content and meaning.

These assorted interpretations or meanings of experience are filed in memory. Later they may be recalled to connect with other meanings or, perhaps, edited in the light of a more recent experience. These meanings provide the substance of one's identity, of one's personhood.

It is not enough to experience and to remember. The events of one's life must be connected to give life coherence. These remembered experiences with their meaning are not atomistic units in isolation; rather, they are woven together in a narrative, the story of one's life. What happens in our lives today either continues or interrupts the story we have been telling ourselves about ourselves. Perhaps it is the story we were telling yesterday, or do the roots of this particular vignette reach back into earlier years? Wherever this new event belongs, the human spirit has the capacity to locate its connecting point and weave it into the narrative flow of the person's life. These different narratives in an integrated life are woven together into a person's master story.[4] This master story carries both our identity and the meaning of our lives.

A person's narrative is not limited to present and past experience. Humans have the capacity to envision the future either as an extension of the present or as a new future. And the future created through anticipation feeds back into the present to condition and shape it. Our identity in part is shaped by the vision we hold of the future.

Personal trauma occurs when the events of our lives contradict our expectations and the meaning our story tells. When a contradiction arises, we are forced to reconsider the story we have been telling. These contradictions occur when new experiences do not fit the old story; at that point a crisis of identity and meaning occurs. In addition to trauma, human perceptions and interpretations are ambiguous, incomplete, and changing; these limitations also force us to edit our stories. The editing process often causes a shift in our perception of God, of other people, and of ourselves. Yet this continuous editing makes our story more nearly congruent with reality.

These abstract principles take on flesh and blood when applied to Tom MacGreggor's experience that first Saturday evening. He struggles with a sermon; the phone rings; an old friend talks with him about his ministry and asks questions that cause Tom to reflect on his recent life experience; he feels something akin to shock; because of this initial encounter he turns to his spiritual friend, with whom he talks freely; his life takes a turn toward God. These events were interpreted as the providence of God in Tom's life and began reshaping his identity. His life took a new turn because his old story had become disconnected from his actual experience; he began editing his story to integrate his actual experience into his master narrative.

Perhaps these capacities of the human psyche make spirituality possible. These abilities are used by all persons to construct a life story. These faculties form the human capacity for true spirituality. In light of these spiritual capacities, each of us has the ability to notice the action of God, to give it definition, to ascribe meaning to it, and to relate it to a larger constellation of meaning in our lives. These created capacities enable humans to have spiritual experience, to translate it, and to shape their lives by its meaning. What is unique about pastoral spirituality—or Christian spirituality, for that matter? In Christian spirituality the person understands his or her life in light of the normative event of God revealed in Jesus Christ. The individual story is interpreted and understood in light of the story of God in Jesus Christ.

Spirituality as Encounter with the Divine

Holmes describes spirituality as "a capacity for relationship with that which transcends sense phenomena."

There is another element in the spiritual matrix—the presence of God. This basic, diadic relationship between God and human beings gives birth to spirituality: God calls us. The initiative, the encounter, and the transformation that occur when the Holy God's call meets human consciousness is the dynamic that generates spirituality in the minister. This grasp of the Holy on human consciousness creates a new center, a new standpoint from which the subject views life. God enters human consciousness and becomes for that individual a centering power.

A person's belief structure determines in large measure how and to what extent God can be noticed. For example, it makes a great deal of difference whether God is a personal presence or an impersonal principle, whether God is wholly other and visits as a stranger or is intimately involved in the daily affairs of a person's life.

Because the faith of the pastor is of such importance, it is imperative to identify certain characteristics of the God who comes to us. First, the God described in scripture wills to be known, to enter into conscious human experience. If God did not will to be known, then the Holy One would remain a mystery, hidden, out of reach. But the creation, the revelation to Israel, and the church testify that God has unmasked a portion of the mystery. The Eternal One has come into our midst through Jesus who is called the Christ.

The writer of John's Gospel states: "And the Word became flesh and dwelt among us, full of grace and truth; we have beheld his glory, glory as of the only Son from the Father. . . . No one has ever seen God; the only Son, who is in the bosom of the Father, he has made him known" (John 1:14, 18). In Christ, God became approachable, vulnerable, visible, touchable.

Had God remained in divine aloneness we would have no choice but to remain in ours. We do not have the power to initiate a relationship with God. But the revelation of God in Christ declares that God wills to be in relationship with us, to be known by us, and to receive our worship, praise, and obedience.

God is person; God has all the capacities of human beings. God is not a thing, not an individual who sits out on the rim of the cosmos. Yet there is no way to experience God except as personal. God comes to us as an "I." God speaks to us, making us a "Thou." In the Genesis account of creation God said, " 'Let there be light'; and there was light" (Gen. 1:3). The story continues: "Then the LORD God formed man of dust from the ground, and breathed into his nostrils the breath of life; and man became a living being" (Gen. 2:7). "And the LORD God commanded the man, saying, 'You may freely eat of every tree of the garden; but of the tree of the knowledge of good and evil you shall not eat, for in the day that you eat of it you shall die' " (Gen. 2:16–17). After the fall into sin the Lord God called to the man, "Where are you?" (Gen. 3:9). In this Word of God to human beings the relationship was created, and in their disobedience humans became estranged. Whenever spirituality loses the element of a personal relationship with God, it degenerates into pantheism or quietism. The personal God wills to be known as a personal presence in every human being.

God is also love—Holy Love. In Christ, we encounter the personal God who wills to be known as love. It is a love that accepts the unacceptable, forgives the sinful, manifests itself in justice. It is a tough, multidimensional love that can be hard when demanding equality and inclusiveness.

The enduring symbol of this love is a cross. Through the ages Christians have seen the cross as representative of God who identified with us and took the worst we had to offer. God took our rejection to show us the depths of the divine love.

In the letter to the Romans, Paul expresses this love:

> While we were still weak, at the right time Christ died for the ungodly. Why, one will hardly die for a righteous man—though perhaps for a good man one will dare even to die. But God shows his love for us in that while we were yet sinners Christ died for us.
>
> Romans 5:6–8

The God who meets us is purposive; God wills and accomplishes what God wills. Through encounter the God of love and power creates in persons an alternative reality. It is a third world of possibility that is ambiguous, playful, slippery, and unpredictable. The encounter with God provides another way of seeing, a vision: not a spiritual world behind the natural world but a vision of the real world and of the final outcome in which a Holy God prevails through love. It is a vision of God's will being done on earth, as it is in heaven. It is a vision of love and justice where all are one and demonstrate that they are children of God. And God is known by all and knows all. The kingdom is indeed God's purpose.

Tom MacGreggor, awakened to the emptiness of his life, is pursuing a deeper awareness of his relation to God. Imagine him at his desk reflecting on his faith and trying to write a credo. Perhaps his initial draft would read like this.

A Personal Credo

I believe in God who has been revealed through the Spirit in Jesus' life.

I believe that God wills to be known by me and thus comes to me, calls me, and changes me.

I believe God knows all there is to know about me but loves me in spite of my sin, ambiguity, and confusion.

I believe God has a purpose for my life. God has chosen me, sustained me, and directed me and will continue to make my life's plan clear to me.

I believe God entered my consciousness in a new form last Saturday night and has awakened my interest and concern.

I believe God will abide with me and will provide me companions for my journey.

Holmes's definition suggests that spirituality is experienced by the subject as "an expanded or heightened consciousness." This awareness is not the result of mental manipulation. It comes as a gift, at times quite unexpected. This expanded awareness speaks of a new center of consciousness, one which has the power to reorient a person's life.

Spirituality, according to Holmes, is "given substance in the historical setting." This element of his definition rescues the word "spiritual" from a gnostic escapism that avoids contact with historical realities. Jim Councilman did not understand the relation between the experience of God and life in the world. The historical substance must include the relationships one has in the church, the stage of life one is in, and the social context in which ministry occurs. Without this connectedness, spirituality becomes private, irrelevant, and self-deceiving.

The Role of Church

The spirituality Tom seeks cannot be created in isolation from other believers. Authentic spirituality is created in the context of a spiritual community. The spiritual community, the church, is like the audience in the arena. (We have already acknowledged the excessive individualism as a glaring weakness in the metaphor.) The crowd is there supporting, encouraging, and identifying with the wrestler. So the minister's spirituality cannot be formed like an egg in a shell in a carton; the egg must be taken out, broken open, and stirred in with other ingredients. In a fashion, the minister's life must be united with the lives of others in the community of faith. This is the meaning of *koinonia,* a participation and sharing in the lives of others.

Participation in the spiritual community is essential because this community keeps the sacred texts, the primal sources of God's revelation. This record provides the norm for the life of faith. This inspired story nourishes the Spirit in the minister and provides the material from which the community lives.

In addition to the record, the community of faith has developed a liturgy that enacts the gospel events, it has rituals for the celebration of the Christian year, and it has symbols and sacraments that point beyond themselves to the Ultimate in being and power. Through participation in these symbolic celebrations, the members of the community recall the past and re-create its meaning in the present to the glory of God and the enrichment of their lives.

The community, along with carrying the record and providing the liturgy, rituals, and symbols, offers a context for relationships. Relations with other journeyers provide support for struggles, offer the energy for which the kingdom of God calls, and serve as a corrective for the interpretation of the presence of the Holy God in human history.

In the community, also, persons tell their stories. The hearers clarify the meaning of the tale; they affirm, correct, and help the storytellers relate their stories to *the* story. The faith community spreads the master narrative like a canopy, and its shadow forms the superstructure of individual stories. Without the larger story, personal narratives lack coherence, direction, and ultimate meaning.

In the community of faith the framework for spirituality precedes the minister. It existed in the corporate memory of the community before the modern minister entered it. This structure for spirituality is reenacted in the rituals of worship, Holy Communion, and the celebrations of the church year. Thus the spirituality in which the minister participates was communal before it was individual. The minister's spirituality is, therefore, a participatory spirituality mediated through a historical community; it is personal because each brings his or her personal story into the community to be affirmed, corrected, and related to God's story. Through this communal telling, each personal story is an individualized version of the master story of God.

If the church is a community of nurture and re-creation, what happened to Tom MacGreggor? As a minister Tom was *in* the congregation but not *of* the congregation. He knew the scriptures, but they had become a source for preaching rather than nurture to his soul. The liturgy and rituals had died in his hands so that the touch of holy things did not stir him. In this state of depletion Tom had drawn back from members of the community who could have helped him.

Time, an Element in Spiritual Growth

The fourth element in the matrix, and an expression of historical substance that develops spirituality, is time. Time is the limiting and structuring factor.

Time, like the ropes around the wrestling ring, creates limits. For each person there is a beginning and an end. The time between the beginning and the end is the time for decision, "my" time. The bell rings at birth, and the bell sounds the closing round. This limitation of time fills "my" time with intensity, value, and responsibility. Because time has this limit, the right time for decision is always now.

Time also provides a feeling of movement in our life story—before and after. The philosopher speaks of the relation of time and motion. Movement creates our sense of time. The movement of the earth upon its axis marks a day. This primal movement gives birth to the notion of time. Conceivably, all time originates from the idea of a day. The extension of time is the multiplication of days into weeks, months, years, decades, millennia, and eons; the briefer units of time are constituted from the division of a day into hours, minutes, seconds, moments, thoughts. The encounter with God occurs in "now time" and colors both memory (past time) and hope (future time).

To give spirituality its proper significance, we must recognize that the "eternal now" is God's time. In Book One of his *Confessions,* Augustine portrays this idea:

No matter how many have already been our days and the days of our fathers, they have all passed through this single present day of yours, and from it they have taken their measures and their manner of being. And others still shall also pass away and receive their measures and their manner of being. "But you are the Selfsame," and all things of tomorrow and all beyond, and all things of yesterday and all things before, you shall make into today, and you have already made them into today.[5]

Today God meets, calls, and transforms us. The development of pastoral spirituality occurs in this now time. In many of us there is a strange sense that our spirituality should be formed by yesterday, an old form; therefore, we seek to escape from the present by a projection of vain expectations upon the future, or we try to impose an incongruent form from the past upon present experience. Neither of these works. We meet God in the unformed moment with openness to new and different manifestations of grace.

We meet God in the present moment, in the context of our real life, whether it is beautiful, faithful, joyous, mundane, painful, or empty. God is to be found in the moment in the present experience. In accepting who we are, in turning toward God in simple surrender, in letting life be whatever it is in the moment, we claim our relation with God through faith and find meaning.

This encounter with the Holy creates meaning for us, but what is meaningful history for God? When God's will is done on earth as it is in heaven, when the human family loves God and loves the neighbor, meaningful history is being created. The consequence of these moments remains in the memory of God forever. God is fulfilled and glorified through the creature's conscious response of love and trust.

Time has value for us humans in a secondary sense only. *Now* is for the fulfillment and glory of God; *now* is the time for doing God's will, for the kingdom to come on earth as it is in heaven. Secondarily, my time includes the maturing of life, actualizing my potential, and finding myself by losing myself in the will of God.

Where will Tom MacGreggor find God? In the emptiness of his life, in the brokenness of his self-confidence, in this moment of honest inquiry. He does not need to go to another church; he does not need to feign a superficial spirituality; he does not need to feel a peculiar emotion; he needs only to open himself to God, who comes to him with grace through the pain and emptiness he feels. If he can only believe it, this emptiness is at the moment the shape of his spirituality, the substance out of which a vital life with God is formed. This "stuff" is the donkey upon which he rides.

The Social Context

Now for another aspect of the historical substance of our spirituality. It is developed not only in the context of spiritual community in time but in the context of the larger society. The shape of spirituality is determined also by the context in which it expresses itself. Holmes has said that spirituality is "given substance in the historical setting, and exhibits itself in creative action in the world." The societal context is like the world outside the arena in which the wrestling match is staged. The world must feel the result of the struggle of our lives; what happens in the ring affects the wrestler's behavior outside the ring. Some in the larger society will choose to participate in the struggle; others will ignore it altogether. Spirituality never flourishes as an escapism isolated from history. A vital spirituality nurtured in a community of faith must be expressed in the larger society. Both our corporate and personal spirituality must address the oppressed, the poor and powerless, the dispossessed, and the discriminated against. God calls for justice and compassion; both we and the community must heed this call.

Our personal piety, the experience of the Holy One, the vision of the kingdom, and the fellowship of the spiritual community must be given concrete embodiment in deeds of compassion and humble service. Pastoral spirituality hears the challenge issued to the rich young man who came to Jesus and was told, "Go, sell what you possess and give to the poor . . . and come, follow me" (Matt. 19:21).

Pastoral spirituality requires an intimate knowledge of oneself, a thorough exploration of one's interiority; but this depth of knowledge must not turn into narcissism. The minister seeks a way to the center of the self to meet God; at the center we open ourselves to the Holy God; from this encounter with God arises a vision of the kingdom of God. Vision enables ministers to labor on with the patient expectancy that was modeled in Abraham. "For he looked for a city which has foundations, whose builder and maker is God" (Heb. 11:10, paraphrased).

> In hope he believed against hope, that he should become the father of many nations; as he had been told, "So shall your descendants be." He did not weaken in faith when he considered his own body, which was as good as dead because he was about a hundred years old, or when he considered the barrenness of Sarah's womb. No distrust made him waver concerning the promise of God, but he grew strong in his faith as he gave glory to God, fully convinced that God was able to do what he had promised.
>
> Romans 4:18–21

Tom MacGreggor must become silent enough to hear God. It is necessary for him to engage the center which has no circumference, to hear the voice of God which speaks in silence, to let that voice give birth to images of hope which portend a new world. And the ministers who have been to the center will engage the structures of society with keener perception; they will see the outline of the will of God in the events of history and will join God in the world.

Destiny

The final element in the spirituality matrix is that of destiny. Although destiny is not mentioned by Holmes, it is the unique part that each person and social unit plays in the fulfillment of history. Destiny is future and beckons us toward it; destiny is a guidance system enabling us to intuit meaning in the present. Destiny finds its home theologically in election, providence, and predestination. The very suggestion of these foundational doctrines fortifies destiny with a certainty and strength that entices us to pursue it with unflagging vigor.

Our destiny has its source in God's election, the free, gracious choice of God for us before the foundation of the world.

> Blessed be the God and Father of our Lord Jesus Christ, who has blessed us in Christ with every spiritual blessing in the heavenly places, even as he chose us in him before the foundation of the world, that we should be holy and blameless before him. He destined us in love to be his sons through Jesus Christ, according to the purpose of his will, to the praise of his glorious grace which he freely bestowed on us in the Beloved.
>
> Ephesians 1:3–6

Election came to us before there was an individual or a community, an inside or an outside, a past or a future. What stronger foundation for the pastor's spirituality could there be than the fact that the minister has been elected by God?

Predestination is written into the structure of our being; it is our identity, who we are. As John Sanford has said, "There is something within us that knows who we are and what we are to do." This belief does not commit us to a passive reception of events in our personal or corporate life; rather, it attracts us toward the future with a certainty that strengthens our efforts. Election and predestination are doctrines that are best realized in retrospect.

Providence suggests the gracious interventions of God in the affairs of our lives. These occurrences are not open to scientific investigation; but in our meeting of certain persons, and in the experience of open doors, inspirations, nudges, and sudden flashes of vision, we see God's hand in our lives. The revelation of God's will gives glimpses of assurance; it calls for decision. Perhaps the providence of God is realized most often through open doors of opportunity. While predestination is retrospective, providence is prospective.

When, therefore, a minister has been called by God, there stands behind that minister the eternal election of God, the effectual calling, and the gracious providence of God, which will empower the called one to do and be what God has intended.

More than a month went by after Tom talked with his spiritual guide. During the intervening weeks he gave a great deal of thought to the elements that make for a vital, holistic spirituality. He was eager to talk to Jesse again, to express his thoughts to someone who understood.

"Well," the old minister began, "what are the contours of a healthy pastoral spirituality?"

"Right at the center," Tom responded, "is my consciousness of God and my response to the divine initiatives in my life. What has happened to me over the past weeks has been like a divine invasion of my awareness."

Jesse nodded in agreement. "What pitfalls must you watch for?"

"I believe that both the divine and the human are essential in this relation. If I focus on myself, my powers and my initiatives, my spirituality will become little more than a refined, narcissistic humanism; if I focus wholly on the divine, it will become a new gnosticism with special knowledge and technique."

"And what of your relation to the fellowship of the church?"

Tom had wondered about this himself. "I am both a giver and a receiver. In the past I have not found a way to receive from the congregation. I still must discover how to participate without losing my role as leader, how and with whom to share the struggles of my life, and how to stand alone when that is necessary."

"What time is it in your life?" Jesse asked.

"As you know, I was thirty-eight last month. A strange thing has begun to happen. I've begun to think about the end of my life, how much time I have and what I should do with it. I seem to be counting the years not to tell how old I am but how much time I have left to live."

"Not so unusual," his friend responded. "Do you realize the crucial nature of now time? *Now* is where you are! *Now* is the place of meeting!"

Confident that Tom was on the way to discovering a healthy spirituality, Jesse continued his instruction. "Did I ever tell you about the shark and the whale? Both were swimming in the sea when the shark swam up to the whale to engage in conversation.

"As they swam along, the shark said to the whale, 'You are so much older than I, and wiser too. Could you tell me where the ocean is?'

"The whale responded, 'The ocean is what you are in *now.*'

"The shark would not believe it. 'Come on, tell me where the ocean is so I may find it!'

"The whale repeated, 'The ocean is here, now; you are in it.'

"Unbelieving, the shark swam away searching for the ocean.

"The moral is—don't spend too much time looking for God."[6]

Tom mused over the story while they sat in silence. "Perhaps that idea will help me. To know God must inevitably lead me into an active engagement with the issues of the day. I can only embrace a spirituality that manifests itself in the transformation of the world."

"Perhaps I can be of help in sorting out your destiny," Jesse suggested. "You have been called by God to a special role in the church: minister of God. As a person in search of meaning, you have been creating a narrative of your life. Review your story. What seems to be the plot you are living out?

"Look also at the gifts you have. What are the things you like to do? What do you do best? What brings you a sense of fulfillment in God's service? These will give you clues to your destiny.

"And one more thing: What are your dreams for the future? Pay attention to your positive images of the future."

The room was quiet as Tom concentrated on writing down everything his spiritual companion was saying.

"One last thing. The next important task you have is to know yourself. The journey inward is the longest and most treacherous, but it is the only way." The older man spoke with the wisdom of age. "When you come to know yourself as you really are, the knowledge of God will not be far away."

Tom left feeling both eager and afraid, aware that his journey inward would be long, treacherous, exciting—and life-changing. He couldn't wait to get started.

3 Self-Awareness in Pastoral Spirituality

It was 11:30 P.M., and Tom MacGreggor lay in bed wide awake. Margie was already asleep beside him, but for Tom, sleep this night seemed as distant as the sun.

His inability to sleep came from the play he and Margie had attended: *Amadeus,* the story of the boy genius, Wolfgang Amadeus Mozart, and his rival, the older and less talented Antonio Salieri, whose jealousy of the young composer would consume him. In the character of Salieri, Tom had run headfirst into himself. As he lay wide-eyed in bed gazing into the darkness, certain scenes replayed themselves in his mind.

Tom felt the intensity of Salieri's adolescent drive to *be* somebody. Early in the play Salieri recounted his youth: "I wanted *Fame.* . . . I wanted to blaze like a comet across the firmament of Europe! . . . By twelve, I was stumbling about under the poplar trees humming my arias and anthems to the Lord. . . . *'Signore,* let me be a composer!' "[1]

Tom argued with himself. "What is wrong with this passion for composition born of a desire to glorify God? Was fame Salieri's only goal, or could his creations actually glorify God?"

As sleep seemed farther and farther away, another scene came to him with a haunting familiarity: Salieri at age thirty-one, now a composer in the court of Emperor Joseph II of Austria, encounters the youthful Mozart and reluctantly acknowledges his genius. Still Salieri prays passionately to God: "Let your voice enter *me!* Let *me* conduct you!"[2]

"What's wrong with that request?" Tom asked himself. "Hasn't every servant of God longed for his voice to become the voice of God? Why else would I have left the real estate business if not for this?"

These questions faded from Tom's mind as he recalled Salieri's shift from adoration and petition to denunciation. He could feel the bitterness in Salieri's words: "I know my fate. Now for the first time I feel my emptiness as Adam felt his nakedness. . . . Tonight at an inn somewhere in this city stands a giggling child who can put on paper, without actually setting down his billiard cue, casual notes which turn my most considered ones into lifeless scratches.

"*Grazie, Signore!*" Salieri adds sarcastically.[3]

With this exposure of his disdain for the fickle, immoral, and frivolous young composer, Salieri says to the God of Mozart, "And *my* only reward —my sublime privilege—is to be the sole man alive in this time who shall clearly recognize Your Incarnation!"

Tom MacGreggor shivered as he recalled the next moment when Salieri turns his rage against God and cries out, "You are the Enemy! I name Thee now—*Nemico Eterno!*"[4]

The awareness that a man who longed to be the instrument of God could make himself the enemy of God had struck Tom like a naked high-voltage wire. Scene by scene, Tom recalled Salieri's deceit and pretense, his evil plot to kill Mozart. But nothing had hit Tom as powerfully as Salieri's last soliloquy when, as an old man contemplating suicide, he holds a razor in his hand and declares: "I was born a pair of ears and nothing else. It is only through hearing music that I know God exists. Only through writing music that I could worship. . . . All around me men seek liberty for mankind. I sought only slavery for myself. To be owned—ordered—exhausted by an *Absolute*. Music. This was denied me, and with it all meaning."

Salieri continues, speaking to all who will follow in his line as second best: "I will stand in the shadows when you come here to this earth in your turns. And when you feel the dreadful bite of your failures—and hear the taunting of unachievable, uncaring God—I will whisper my name to you: 'Salieri: Patron Saint of Mediocrities!' And in the depth of your downcastness you can pray to me. And I will forgive you."[5]

"Patron Saint of Mediocrities." Tom could not bear the thought. He himself felt the naked emptiness. Had God forsaken him too?

Tom knew it was not the story of Salieri's lust for fame, his professional mediocrity, and later rage against Mozart that kept him sleepless. No. He was aware that a buried part of himself had walked across that stage. In this pretentiously godly man turned demon, Tom had met his own shadow. Given the emptiness of his ministry and his self-doubts, the play disturbed him more than he wished to admit even to himself.

How could he find the courage to come face-to-face with his inner depths when he didn't know what lay there? Elements of the sinister Salieri? Aspects of the genius Mozart? Both?

The next morning Tom rose early and went to his study. Idly glancing across his bookshelf, he spotted an old seminary text, John Calvin's *Institutes of the Christian Religion*. He pulled down the first volume and reviewed a passage he had once committed to memory:

Without knowledge of self there is no knowledge of God. Nearly all the
wisdom we possess, that is to say, true and sound wisdom, consists of
two parts: the knowledge of God and of ourselves. But, while joined
by many bonds, which one precedes and brings forth the other is not
easy to discern. In the first place, no one can look upon himself [sic]
without immediately turning his thoughts to the contemplation of
God, in whom he "lives and moves" (Acts 17:28). For, quite clearly,
the mighty gifts with which we are endowed are hardly from ourselves;
indeed, our very being is nothing but subsistence in the one God. Then,
by these benefits shed like dew from heaven upon us, we are led as by
rivulets to the spring itself.[6]

If Tom intended to know God, he had to look hard at himself. He felt
some resistance to doing so, but if that was a necessary part of his journey,
he would prepare himself. Perhaps the "rivulets" of self-awareness would
lead him "to the spring itself." The notion that knowledge of self and
knowledge of God belong together called up a memorable quotation:
"Therefore strain every nerve in every possible way to know and experience
yourself as you really are. It will not be long, I suspect, before you have a
real knowledge and experience God as [God] is."[7]

Certainly there is no single approach to knowledge of the self, but it is
important to have a way of looking at the self. What are the lenses through
which the self is to be viewed? Carl G. Jung's description of the psyche
provides a variety of approaches to self-knowledge, approaches he spent a
lifetime discovering. "From my eleventh year," he said, "I have been
launched upon a single enterprise which is my 'main business' . . . to
penetrate into the secret of the personality."[8]

This single-minded quest may have been evoked in part by an issue quite
similar to Tom MacGreggor's. As a child Jung asked profound questions
of his father, such as, "How does God relate to the human soul? Where do
persons go when they die?" His father responded with doctrine, which Jung
later discovered the older man questioned. In these early years Jung turned
his attention to the experience *of* God, rather than to dead propositions
about God. This early decision may explain why his picture of the psyche
offers a positive theoretical framework for the development of pastoral
spirituality.

Jung's Description of the Psyche

If self-awareness and God awareness are the foundational elements for
the development of a spirituality, the basic question confronting the pastor
is: "How will I become aware of the various aspects of myself?" Perhaps

a summary of Jung's view of the soul will provide a frame of reference for this self-discovery. (See Figure 2.)

For Jung the soul is a spiritual reality. It is a nonmaterial entity, a reality we must reclaim. According to Jung, the soul possesses three levels of consciousness: personal consciousness, the personal unconscious, and the collective unconscious. These different forms of consciousness contain different kinds of data, yet they are related.

The ego is at the center of consciousness and is comparable to the captain of a ship. It contains the will, with the capacity to direct the individual.

Within a person's consciousness are four functions. First, the functions with which we receive data: intuition and sensation. We either receive data from the inside through intuition or from the outside by sensation.

Once received, consciousness acts upon these data in one of two ways: feeling or thinking. By feeling, Jung means valuing, deciding, and acting. By thinking, he means analyzing, organizing, and structuring. Thus, the second pair of functions.

Though in the figure these functions appear to be related individually to memory, subjective reactions, bodily function, and shadow, in reality each capacity is related to the whole of the personal unconscious and not to one aspect only.

While these four functions are found in all persons, each person has a preference for gathering data: intuition or sensation. Each has a preferred way to operate on the data: feeling or thinking. Preference means that by nature we move in these chosen directions, but preference does not exclude the use of the opposite function; each person uses all four.

According to Jung, each personality is primarily oriented either to the outer world of things and persons or to the inner world of feelings and ideas. This contrast in orientation defines what he means by introversion and extroversion. At the core of this concept is the matter of energy. The extrovert receives energy through relationships and activities in the external world. The inner world is often unknown to the extrovert and may become a source of boredom. The introvert, on the other hand, is energized through solitude and a retreat within. The outer world of relationships and activities drains the introvert of energy and forces a retreat to silence for renewal.

Jung also believed a ground plan was written into our psychic and biological being. This ground plan resembles a genetic coding that directs the individual toward fulfillment. By discerning this ground plan and actualizing it through free choice, persons discover their destiny. Jung called this actualization of the self "individuation."

The persona, a word that means "mask," is the face we show our public. It is produced over the first forty years of life to help us get along in social

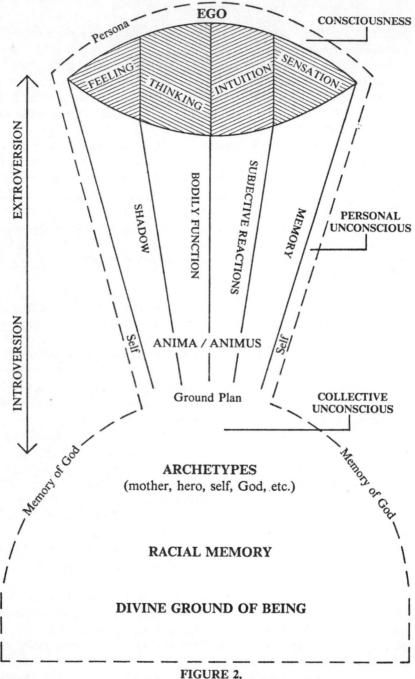

FIGURE 2.
A Jungian view of the soul.

relations. Often the persona develops to meet the expectations of significant other persons in our social world.

Shadow for Jung represents the dark side of our being. It is that part of us of which we are afraid. Since it lurks in the unconscious, it can break into our conscious life with destructive force. Here we are only introducing the Jungian terms. As the reference to *Amadeus* hints, the shadow has great significance for spiritual growth. We will say more about it later.

Jung also recognized in the personal unconscious the potentiality for being, the gifts that persons have by creation, which they are destined throughout their lives to elicit and mature. This view contrasts with that of Freud, who saw the unconscious as a reservoir of negative repressions.

This glossary of terms intends to be an introduction to a few of Jung's seminal concepts that will enable us to discern both the issues and the potential each of us has to grow spiritually.

How do these various functions of the soul enable us to deepen our self-awareness? What are the implications of this view of the soul for self-awareness and the enrichment of the spirit for a minister like Tom MacGreggor, who has been disturbed by his dark side?

The Jungian View of the Soul and of Awareness

Personal consciousness is a uniquely human characteristic. Persons are aware; but they are also aware that they are aware. Self-awareness is awareness turned back upon itself. In the realm of awareness, spirituality develops. This notion we introduced in the matrix.

"I am. I am aware that I am." In those two statements a person can stand outside the self and view it as an object. In this existential awareness four questions are inevitable.

The self in awareness has a consciousness of a before and an after, a history. The question this awareness provokes is: *Where did I come from?* Where did I receive my being? When this question has exhausted the biological, social, and psychic origins, it presses hard the mystery of being. It presses consciousness into mystery.

In the present, this self-transcending awareness asks another question: *Who am I?* In comparison with all other persons and things, what is my uniqueness? This is the question of identity. Identity distinguishes the self from all other selves. Spirituality develops as the person contemplates the ultimate issue of identity: Who am I in relation to God?

The next question this awareness asks is: *Why am I here?* What is the purpose of my being? Without purpose, the self cannot exist. Yet all temporal goals eventually collapse, and the abyss of meaninglessness threatens disruption. Thus the question of purpose demands an answer that transcends the present moment, that even transcends time. The question cannot be fully answered until the purpose of one's life is related to God.

Finally, this self, aware of itself, transcends the present in the direction of the future. Beyond tomorrow, next week, and next year this self can imagine the "no more" of being. In this awareness the self asks, *Where am I going?* Where am I going when time for me no longer exists? How will I be with God, eternally?

The answer to these four existential questions constitutes the substance of one's spirituality. We all ask; we all answer. How a person answers these questions provides the content of the spiritual life. Not to answer these questions is to remain subhuman, repressing the distinctively human issues.[9]

The four functions of consciousness indicate the ways in which God comes to us and the options we have for responding to the divine intervention in our lives. The perceptive functions suggest that awareness of God comes either from the inner world of intuition and imagination or from the external world of sensation. Tom MacGreggor's call to ministry seems to have originated in his own mysterious depths. There were external influences, to be sure, but the call itself came into consciousness in the form of an idea. It appeared as an issue for him to deal with.

Tom's recent experience with his old friend came through the senses: a telephone call; a brief conversation; a seed planted in consciousness that caused him to take a hard look at himself and his ministry.

When these experiences came to him, he had two ways of responding: thinking or feeling. With respect to the call he received from God to become a minister, he had begun with thinking. Why should I become a minister? What will it cost? Will Margie feel the call? In this instance he used analysis, logic, and evaluation in order to respond to God. As for the phone call from his friend, his response was different. There was something in the way Jesse spoke; images of hope had flooded Tom's mind during and after the conversation. He could only describe his response as a hunger for the reality of God in his ministry.

Consciousness is, therefore, the arena of action. Much may occur in the self or in the world, but unless we are aware of the occurrence, it affects our relation to God only slightly. Spirituality arises from the desire and the ability to notice what is happening, to be present to oneself and one's world, and to respond to these data as a person of faith. These data regarding human consciousness underscore the premise that spirituality means a transformation of consciousness.

The Personal Unconscious

The personal unconscious, in contrast to personal consciousness, holds the larger portion of the self. The unconscious resembles the vast extension of the iceberg beneath the surface of the water, while consciousness is like the small portion exposed to the atmosphere. This deeper self contains memory, shadow, and potentiality.

Memory stores all our experiences and their meaning. In this personal depth reside the patterns we have created through developmental crises, the various images of self that have played their part on the stage of our life, and our unresolved conflicts. These memories may be brought to consciousness for resolution, change, and integration.

Through the story of *Amadeus* Tom had a moving experience, an encounter with himself. Naturally, the next day he was capable of recalling the experience and the associated feelings; perhaps with guidance he could identify the experiences he associated with the characters. Though this material was not present in consciousness until called for, memory could bring it to his awareness.

Memory carries the narrative that the ego creates from the substance of the existential questions. This narrative also provides a continuous identity through the stages of life. And when the occasion demands it, the ego can summon this narrative, relate portions of it, and through it relate to others. The narrative both consciously and unconsciously provides a constant sense of self.

The shadow also lurks in the unconscious. Jung has several ways of talking about the shadow. It is the opposite side of our dominant function; it resides in the weak, undeveloped side of our personality to distract or embarrass us; sometimes it breaks into consciousness with destructive force. But the shadow also represents a neglected or separated part of ourselves, a part we do not admit to consciousness. The shadow illuminates the experience Tom MacGreggor had watching *Amadeus.* He unconsciously projected a part of his dark side onto the character of Salieri, who rejected the sovereign will of God and became hostile to the Creator. Salieri's shadow seized his consciousness and caused him to destroy Mozart and attempt to take his own life. Tom identified with this shadow to the extent that he realized a dark side of himself that could, because of jealousy, destroy those persons whose gifts appeared greater than his own.

Within the unconscious dimension of memory, subjective reaction, genetic inheritance as manifested in bodily function, and personal shadow, there reside our untapped possibilities. These potentialities speak to us from the depths through dreams and deep desires, but they must be brought to awareness to be acted upon. Intuition of our destiny rises to the surface of consciousness like vague, thin line drawings of our future, which disappear in the haze but reappear to haunt or to inspire us. This positive view of the unconscious contrasts with Freud, who placed in the unconscious repressed sexual material and negative desires that the superego would not admit to consciousness.

Spirituality grows through actualizing the unconscious potential in the psyche. How does one listen to the suggestions of the unconscious? The deep mind speaks the language of symbol, dream, and metaphor; the material appears in consciousness as intuitions and hunches. If we wish to pick up the signals sent by the unconscious, we must cultivate the habit of listening to our soul. Of course, illusions are possible! But it is also possible to hear God.

The Collective Unconscious

According to Jung, each of us also participates in a collective unconscious. The collective unconscious is more remote than the personal unconscious; it is more general, impersonal, and contains images that are transpersonal. The collective unconscious is the heritage of the race, with layers of mythological motifs, racial memories, and archetypes. These archetypes refer to patterning tendencies of relating common human experiences. These forms in the racial memory constitute the cast of characters who play different roles in the drama of every culture of every generation. In *Amadeus,* for example, the two characters, Mozart and Salieri, play out the archetypes of Hero and Dragon.

The Ego

The ego, for Jung, selects and relates as the center of consciousness. It possesses the will to choose its own direction. As an example, when data come into consciousness either through sensation or intuition, it is the ego that must decide what to do with them. If the person chooses to think about, analyze, and organize the data into a systematic whole, the ego makes that choice.

When the ego becomes inflated, it tends to operate disconnected from its data. Recall Salieri's confession: "I wanted Fame. . . . I wanted to blaze like a comet across the firmament of Europe!" Here is an ego gone mad. The desire stems from a hunger for recognition beyond the capacities of the person.

The ego can make choices that are in harmony with one's nature and gifts. The ego can elect the direction in which life is lived. For example, the Christian believer seeks to make choices according to the mind and will of Christ. Christ said, "If anyone chooses to be my disciple, let him say 'no' to himself, put the cross on his shoulders daily and keep on following me" (Luke 9:23, paraphrased).

In discovering the ego, the questions to ask are: What have I chosen? What do I value? In what directions am I moving? What are my loyalties? Have these decisions been influenced by Christ?

The Persona

The persona does not represent the self. Rather, it is the identity a person creates to meet the cultural demands. The persona is the mask each individual creates in an effort to comply with the expectations of others. The persona originates from outside: that is, it is our behavioral response to gain social acceptance and enable us to function in our relationships. The persona provides a functional identity. To develop an authentic self, and thus an authentic spirituality, each person must become aware of the persona. The persona projects an identity but not one that is congruent with the true being of the person. Becoming aware of the persona and beginning the process of dismantling it is both a painful and a threatening experience.

Our brief look at Tom MacGreggor suggests that he may be getting involved in this process. He is becoming aware of his desire to please his congregation; he recognizes that he has vain ambitions, which if achieved would enable him to measure up to an image he holds of himself. At times he feels that his words and responses do not come from his heart; he seems to be playing a role rather than being a minister of Jesus Christ. Perhaps his persona is coming unstuck, and he stands on the verge of authenticity.

Jung says we spend the first forty years creating the persona. We will not forsake it easily. Two questions can help a person begin identifying the persona: What is the face I seek to show? How is it different from what I know myself to be?

Individuation

At the center of Jung's understanding of the psyche lies his concept of individuation. To him, individuation means becoming an individual, becoming one's own self. Scientifically, it refers to "a biological process . . . by which every living thing becomes what it was destined to be from the beginning."[10]

The drive toward individuation is inherent in the organism and presses for the actualization of the ground plan written in the psyche. This drive, which has its origin in the unconscious, seeks to make the individual conscious of his or her gifts, potentialities, and options. These intuitions received and actualized in concrete choices constitute the unfolding of a person's life.

Another of Jung's concepts closely related to individuation is that of the personal story. According to Jung, each of us is living a narrative; the story we tell with our lives is the narrative of our individuation.

Jung first noticed the role of narrative in dealing with psychotic individuals. He was treating a woman who had been in a deep psychosis for a number of years. She continued to make a series of motions that resembled those of a cobbler. In consultation with her brother, who came to visit her, Jung discovered that she had had a painful break with a man who was a cobbler. He concluded that behind all psychosis there is a story. "To my mind," he said, "therapy only really begins after the investigation of that wholly personal story. It is the patient's secret, the rock against which [the patient] is shattered."[11] Jung sees the story as the crucial element in a person's life because it contains "a personality, a life history, a pattern of hopes and desires [that] lie behind the psychosis."[12]

Not only is this true of persons with psychoses; each of us is a story. As already emphasized in the matrix, our lives constitute a narrative we are telling ourselves about the things that have happened to us. In order to understand ourselves, we must examine the story we are telling with our lives.[13]

This Jungian model provides a variety of ways to look at ourselves. The collection of these data provides a composite picture of who we are. According to Calvin, each aspect of our knowledge of self throws us more completely upon the mercy of God: that is, a deepening knowledge of self drives us to an expanded knowledge of God. Thus, self-knowledge and the knowledge of God are intrinsically bound. Spirituality consists of our knowledge of self and our knowledge of God fused together.

A Jungian Spirituality

What is the shape of a spirituality that is formed by the capacities of the soul as set forth by Jung? If spirituality is the encounter of the self with God, Jung's model suggests that God may approach the self from within, through intuition, or from without, through sensation. The awareness of God may be reflected on (thinking) or responded to in loving action or devotion (feeling). These functions define types of prayer as a meditative listening to one's depths or an active discernment of God in providence, for one example.

This model suggests several tasks of spiritual growth. To become a whole authentic person requires the dismantling of a false self, the persona. Is this not what Jesus referred to when he said, "If any man would come after me, let him deny himself"? He calls us to deny the false self that would "blaze like a comet across the firmament of Europe."

Another task is the cleansing of the unconscious by the exposure of our guilty and painful memories to an all-wise and loving God. These unacceptable parts of ourself rise to haunt us unless cleansed through confession. The Augustinian type of confession of one's whole life has enormous healing potential.[14]

Jung's model indicates the necessity of dealing with the dark side, the shadow aspect of our personality. The shadow differs from painful, repressed memories; it is unconscious and beyond the reach of memory. The shadow manifests itself in behavior that betrays Christ.

The concept of individuation provides an image of growth that attacks the separation of the natural from the spiritual. What any of us will become has roots in our created being. Written into the structure of our psyche is the intention of God. To become what one was created to be unites the natural with the spiritual. To be spiritual, therefore, means to become fully human, not less human. Thus, one does not deny his or her humanity for the sake of spirituality. For those who have understood spirituality as being other than oneself, the repudiation of self, or the substitution of Christ for the self, this image of spirituality offers a welcome affirmation.

The Jungian model of the soul offers a needed corrective to a humanistic, scientific worldview. The construct of the personal unconscious opens the psyche to Mystery. It acknowledges the presence of images, ideas, and intuitions that appear in consciousness without apparent cause, thus ruling out a cause-and-effect explanation. Positing this mysterious depth of the ground plan and human potential allows room for the Creator to act within the unconscious long before this activity breaks into consciousness. Perhaps the God of Mystery constantly bathes our unconscious depths as the ocean's waves wash the shore.

This way of viewing the self issues an invitation to adventure. The mysterious depth of the psyche, which holds all the potential for our becoming, is constantly exposed to the divine invasion. Through the energizing presence of the Holy One, spontaneous images break the silence of consciousness, capture our attention, inspire visions of the future, and lure each of us toward human fulfillment . . . and the fulfillment of the eternal purpose of God.

We left Tom MacGreggor in the study contemplating the knowledge of self and the knowledge of God. Alarmed by the projection of himself into the behavior of Salieri, he had turned to Calvin's *Institutes* to discover the necessity for a knowledge of himself.

Suppose that Tom MacGreggor had discovered the seminal concepts in Jung. Would his fear of becoming the "Patron Saint of Mediocrities" drive him to examine his own depths? How would Tom respond to a call to examine his persona, his ministerial face? Or to examine his ego, which also wishes that God would possess him and speak through him? Would he have the courage to look at his shadow, of which he has become aware but of whose power he does not know?

Listen to the conversation that takes place in Tom's head as he struggles with these issues.

"I know that the knowledge of God, at least in part, depends on a knowledge of myself. To resist this knowledge is to resist God. I wish to know both myself and God, but at the same time I am afraid to know.

"Why am I afraid to know myself?" Tom wondered aloud. "Am I afraid that if I explore my inner self, I won't find anything? Do I fear that my own depths are like a dark, damp basement with bare walls, cobwebs, dry rot, and nothing else?"

Perhaps the dark image of Salieri left a different picture in Tom's mind. "If I open my depths, I may discover a monster that I have sealed off from my awareness for years. What if I let him out and he tries to destroy me?

"If I do not take the risk," Tom reasoned, "I will never know."

He is right. Beneath the surface of consciousness lies the vast potential for his ministry, his personal growth, and the energy he sorely lacks at present. He has gifts, capacities, and possibilities for ministry that he has only slightly begun to exploit. To discover them, he must live the adventure into the unknown. At age thirty-eight Tom has constructed a world in which he finds comfort and a degree of meaning. He feels accepted by his congregation; his marriage is stable.

"What if," Tom asked himself, "I engage the world of spirit and this changes me? Am I ready for an interruption in my life? Such a change might introduce a new and different world. This radical shift could call my identity into question. Am I strong enough to withstand this tidal wave of change?"

These fears filled Tom's mind that morning as he considered the journey into his depths. Did he dare to know himself . . . and God?

Sources of Strength

We all share Tom MacGreggor's questions and fears. Some few may begin the adventure out of fascination, but most risk engagement with their depths because of the pain in their lives. As we contemplate the long and fearful journey into the self, we are not left alone to deal with our fears. We are supported. Christ has promised to be with us always. No one makes the journey into the depths alone. "Though I walk through the valley of the shadow of death, thou art with me." We can affirm a presence.

Christ intends our wholeness, not our destruction. "I have come that you might have life and that you might have it more abundantly" (John 10:10, paraphrased). Christ has said, "He who has my commandments and keeps them, it is he who loves me; and he that loves me will be loved of my Father, and we will come into him and make our abode with him" (John 14:21, 23, paraphrased). Scripture says, "The light shines in the darkness, and the darkness cannot overcome it" (John 1:5, paraphrased). Christ purposes to bring to light the hidden things of darkness and to make them manifest in the light of the Father's love.

Christ has the power to sustain us when the monster within us breaks loose, when the structure gives way, when the mask falls off, when our weaknesses are realized and exposed, and when our story is interrupted. Christ will walk with us through the deep, dark corridors of our soul and will restore us to wholeness and life.

Are we prepared for the adventure?

4 Pastoral Spirituality as Process

Returning from another session with Jesse, Tom drove down Route 1 feeling relieved at having shared with his spiritual guide the new personal insights he had gained. He didn't particularly like what he was finding, but facing himself honestly gave him a degree of freedom and hope. The new freedom he was experiencing gave him the courage to keep at the task.

This inward journey upon which he was embarking disputed Tom's somewhat naive understanding of the Christian life. Even in his adult years, he had seen the faith in fairly clear categories: true or false, right or wrong, in or out of the faith. His first steps into his own psyche challenged these assumptions. Honesty forced him to admit that his own life was a mixture of trust and doubt, of autonomy and dependence, of ambition and inferiority. Did this ambiguity invalidate his faith, his relation to Christ?

As he drove through a countryside made green by spring, he wondered at a statement Jesse had made. "Life is a journey, not a destination; it is a process of change, not a utopia. You will always be on the road and under canvas, tenting like a pilgrim!" These images created both doubt and curiosity: doubt about his old ways of looking at the Christian life and curiosity about the new possibilities hidden in the ideas of "journey," "process," "on the road."

Life as a process or journey offered him a metaphor of Christian development that not only explained his ambiguity but challenged him to recognize the constant movement in his life. He recognized how time, as a key element in the spiritual matrix, precipitated changes both inside and outside. These changes challenged, and would continue to challenge, his well-defined formulations of the faith; the dissonance between confession and realization explained his ambiguity.

The phrase Jesse used kept running through his mind: "On the road and under canvas." The image made sense. His life had been one of process and unfolding. From his early days in a small town right up to being pastor of

Greystone Church, he had found no permanent dwelling; life had consisted of raising the tent of world perception only to take it down in order to move on to new images and concepts.

Tom could not prevent a smile as his thoughts were interrupted by a song blaring from the car radio: Willie Nelson's "On the Road Again." He reached over and flipped off the sound. At the moment he needed quiet more than entertainment, stability more than change.

As Tom drove in silence, symbols of his life process began appearing along the road: a cow with a new calf, green leaves and new blades of grass, a shock of corn left from the fall, a man and woman with two children passing in a new car, a cemetery. In time he too would pass through all the stages from birth to maturity to death, and certainly God was in that process. But how could he grasp the ways in which God came to him? How could he respond to the invitations of God in the unfolding drama of his life?

These questions served as a magnet in Tom's memory to draw into consciousness an eventful weekend during his seminary days. The Dean had announced that Interpreter's House had invited a dozen seminarians and their spouses for a conference on pastoral development. Thomas Louis MacGreggor had been chosen to participate.

Dr. Carlyle Marney, the founder and resident guru at Interpreter's House, guided the sessions. On Saturday morning he gave each participant a mimeographed copy of Erik Erikson's "Eight Ages of Man."[1] At the time Tom was impressed with the psychosocial theory of personal development; he saw how it could help him in counseling, but it never occurred to him that this time-controlled development offered a structure for his own spiritual life.

As he drove, Tom recalled a number of the categories with which Erikson dealt, so he applied them to himself.

Do I have a basic trust in the goodness of God and of life?

Have I a sense of autonomy that enables me to function independently?

How do my frequent feelings of inferiority relate to my not having been affirmed as a child? Does this lie at the base of my concern that God does not accept my offering of service?

Why do I often feel confused about my personal identity? Why do I confuse the role of the minister with my personal identity?

Why am I afraid to surrender myself wholly to God? Where do the fears of losing myself come from?

Has my recent experience of burnout been precipitated or fueled by failed crises in my personal development?

Tom recognized that in some way these questions were related to what Jesse had said: "Life is a journey and not a destination." His next challenge would be to discover that spirituality is also a process.

Life Is a Journey

Pastoral spirituality is a dynamic process; it cannot be frozen, and it offers no final utopia, no feeling of having arrived. Utopia literally is "no place," despite our deep yearning to find a place of final rest where change does not threaten. The hunger for rest finds satisfaction only in living the changes, not avoiding them. We are always "on the road and under canvas."

Like a journey in which the landscape constantly changes, life continually confronts us with new challenges within and without. As these internal changes occur, they precipitate shifts in one's vision of self and of God. If one's spirituality is alive and relevant, it will also be in process.

This idea of change finds legitimacy in the scriptures. The Bible recognizes the developmental nature of life. In the first epistle of John, the author addressed children, young men, and old men (1 John 2:12–14). Doubtless he discerned that their comprehension had various levels of sophistication, and the gospel had different applications for each of the stages of life. The apostle addressed each group, recognizing the necessity for speaking the Word of God in the context of the hearers' needs and understanding.

The stories of Jesus also suggest an awareness of development. The seed, for example, first sprouts; then it sends forth the blade, next the ear and, finally, the full ear of grain (Mark 4:28). Jesus' stories indicate his awareness of different modes of consciousness, as when he spoke of the ground receiving the seed in different ways. Some soil was packed hard, some soil was overrun with weeds, and some was good soil. These different kinds of soil compare to different modes of consciousness. Consciousness receives the seed in contrasting ways: insensitively, superficially, wholeheartedly. At different stages of development, human consciousness has variety in the ways it receives the Word of God.

Our task is to find a way to look at our own development and that of other persons in order to understand how the Word of God influences life at different stages, how it issues invitations in our development. One helpful source to guide us in this task is the theoretical work of Erik Erikson, a developmental psychologist.

Before introducing Erikson's developmental schema, let me remind the reader of our point of view. We are presupposing the creation, the re-creation, and the call of God in the life of the minister. These theological realities provide the foundation for an examination of natural psychological development. Our perspective does not assume that a person who successfully negotiates the various stages of development automatically achieves a Christian conversion; the development of various personality strengths does not substitute for hearing the gospel and responding to Christ. On the other hand, how persons hear the Word of God and their capacities for response have been shaped by the manner in which these developmental stages have been negotiated. Stated theologically, the grace of God builds upon nature, judges and refines nature, but neither ignores nor destroys nature! God both created and redeemed us; these two mighty acts must not be separated.

A Developmental Framework for Pastoral Spirituality

The developmental schema of Erik Erikson provides an appropriate framework for envisioning developmental spiritual crises and thus the tasks of a developing spiritual person. It is our intention to examine each of Erikson's stages and listen to the invitation to spiritual growth in each.

Perhaps the best way to approach the Erikson theory is with a statement of the epigenetic principle. Erikson says that "anything that grows has a ground plan, and that out of this ground plan the parts arise, each part having its time of special ascendancy, until all parts have arisen to form a functioning whole."[2]

The human organism grows according to a ground plan that is written into the structure of its being. Out of the ground plan the different parts arise, and each has its special time of emphasis or development until the organism forms a whole. Erikson employs this biological principle as a model for psychosocial development. Persons not only develop bodies but basic attitudes, confidences, images of self, and competencies to act in human relations and in the larger social environment. This series of psychic developments shapes the recipient of God's grace.

As the physical organism—the human body—develops, different parts have their ascendancy until it is fully functioning. Each stage in bodily development and uses of the body (and their decline) triggers a series of changes that affect identity, the relation with significant persons, competency, and a perspective on life.

Consider how this constellation of influences associated with development works in actual fact. A baby girl, for example, does not possess control over her body and therefore depends upon adults to feed and clothe her, bathe her, and care for her in every way. The significant relation at this stage is with the maternal person; the identity of the infant is fused with that of the mother. Through this relation the infant assumes a basic posture toward life of either trust or mistrust.

Contrast the six-year-old girl with the infant. A number of physical advances have made possible locomotion, coordination, and a growing independence. The maternal relation has enlarged to include both parents, teachers, and, perhaps, the minister. The infant has now established herself as a separate person with the ability to make things like toy houses and pictures. This little individual now has a firmer sense of self, though not a fully developed one. The competency she develops in making things will later be useful in handling responsibility. The child's concept of God is usually quite literal, having the character of the dominant parent. How the infant relates to the dominant parent, the consequent notion of the world she derives, and the competency with which the six-year-old functions in leaving Mother or making things—all these shape how she hears God's call. Since growth and change end only with death, the constant changes in one's self and one's environment continue to precipitate a shift in the relation with God.

To understand spirituality as a process, we emphasize that one's whole life consists of the continuous composing and recomposing of a perspective, "always on the road and under canvas." From infancy to old age these changes occur with predictable regularity, and each affects the person— one's significant relations and one's relation with God. Our task is first to identify these stages and then to explore the implications of the changes for pastoral spirituality. Perhaps it is important to underscore at the outset that different stages signal the recomposing of our own relation to God. Recomposing suggests forming images and relations in a different way, refining, repairing, adding sophistication. Like a composer who writes an étude and returns to make changes, or a writer who rewrites an essay, we too live the process of adapting our lives to the realities of our situation.

Erikson constructs this theory of psychosocial development with a keen observation of the social context as a major influence. Development for Erikson occurs in the tension between the self and its social environment, with its positive and negative forces from which the person seeks to achieve a favorable ratio: that is, a balance of the opposing forces, like trust vs. mistrust. Through the resolution of the tension in each of these stages, the individual develops a series of competencies or virtues that facilitate positive relations in his or her social world. To fail in the resolution of these crises cripples the functioning of the developing person. How these issues are resolved directly affects how a person relates to God.

In the process of development, a person may fail to achieve a favorable ratio, get stuck in a particular stage, or regress to an earlier stage. These aberrations suggest the task of reworking the failures of earlier stages. Since all stages, however, are present in each, each stage provides a setting for accomplishing this task. Those crises that lie behind us are pressing us and giving us strength (unless they were failed crises), and the crises before us impinge upon present decisions.

God in grace accompanies us through the unfolding stages of our lives and invites us into a deeper, and perhaps a more significant, relationship through each crisis. All persons pass through these stages, and the changes within them affect how they perceive both God and themselves. We will look at these stages as they affect the development of the person of a pastor, and at the particular invitations they extend the pastor who is developing an authentic spirituality.

Invitations of the Eight Stages

In order to explore the invitation of each stage to spiritual growth, we will note the primal experience that precipitates the crisis introducing the stage, the strength it produces, the call of God it issues, and how each strength is illustrated in statements of Jesus. Keep in mind that the early patterns we develop continue to inform our personal and spiritual relations. Figure 3 illustrates the eight stages and their relations, virtues, and strengths.[3]

Stage One

The first stage is *basic trust vs. basic mistrust.* In its earliest form, basic trust arises from the relationship with the dominant parent, most often the mother. This relationship provides an orientation to life. The way the mother speaks to the child, holds the child, and is an ever-present figure giving the child's world security provides the experiences from which the child derives a basic sense of trust or mistrust in the order of the world. To say that this infant consciously reasons that life experience can be trusted is not implied. Rather, these experiences form the first thin lines of an attitude toward life, an attitude that is intuited. Once the pattern has been established, later experiences reinforce it like a heavy-leaded pencil tracing over the original outline.

In these earliest experiences the mother calls the infant into awareness and provides an image of the primal God-human relation. Providing for the child's needs, she holds the power of life and death. From this primal relation the child draws the images that will later be used to symbolize God.

Although these primal images, which were unconsciously absorbed before rational development, may be corrected at later stages, the first year forms a basic orientation to the world. The infant learns through these experiences whether to trust or mistrust life. Is it not clear that the earliest experiences predispose one toward life, persons, and the world? This intuitively selected response operates effectively in the child through the early years of development. Later it forms a part of the context in which this person receives the gospel of Christ.

Stated another way, this earliest relationship with the mother forms the pattern that is expressed later in life as faith in God or mistrust in God. This primal experience provides the most basic ingredient in the religious life. Is life to be trusted, especially through the changes? Can God and God's world be trusted?

In Jesus, we see a basic trust in God. He says, "I thank you that you always hear me." And again, "The Father is always with me."

Age	SIGNIFICANT RELATIONS	Stage	Psychosocial Crises	SPIRITUAL CAPACITIES/VIRTUES
75	HUMANKIND MY KIND	VIII	INTEGRITY VS. DESPAIR	UNION WITH GOD/WISDOM
60	DIVIDED LABOR SHARED HOUSEHOLD	VII	GENERATIVITY VS. STAGNATION	STEWARDSHIP/CARE
40	PARTNERS IN FRIENDSHIP SEX, COOPERATION	VI	INTIMACY VS. ISOLATION	COMMITMENT DISCIPLESHIP /LOVE
20	PEER GROUPS, OUT GROUPS MODELS/MENTORS	V	IDENTITY VS. ROLE CONFUSION	IDENTITY WITH CHRIST /FIDELITY
10	NEIGHBORHOOD SCHOOL	IV	INDUSTRY VS. INFERIORITY	GOOD WORKS/COMPETENCE
5	BASIC FAMILY	III	INITIATIVE VS. GUILT	COURAGE TO RISK /PURPOSE
2	PATERNAL PERSONS	II	AUTONOMY VS. SHAME & DOUBT	SELF-AFFIRMATION/WILL
BIRTH	MATERNAL PERSONS	I	BASIC TRUST VS. BASIC MISTRUST	FAITH/HOPE

FIGURE 3.
Psychosocial Crises.

Stage Two

The second Eriksonian crisis is *autonomy vs. shame and doubt.* This crisis arises from the early recognition that one has power "to hold on or let go." With the development of the sphincter muscle, the growing infant begins to control the bowel. Within this matrix the child begins to develop independence and self-control. At this time a distinction arises between self and others. Individuality surfaces as the infant begins to discover what is "me" and "not me." Mother's breast comes and goes; she can be present and then go away. This coming and going provides the first experience of detachment. This separation from the mother provides an emotional distance for the psyche, just as cutting the umbilical cord provided separation from the bearer's body. These early experiences give the developing person a sense of separateness.

The strength that comes from a favorable resolution of this crisis is that of will. It is the ability to express oneself in ways other than the expectations and demands of others. Without the strength of will, a person fears being consumed by society, the group, or another person and is likely to be a compliant individual. A spirituality that can stand alone as a self, but that can also be in community without sacrificing the self, is the strength that arises through this developmental stage.

God's invitation in this stage is to become a distinct person who has control over self. Perhaps the pattern that develops in holding on and letting go offers the first experience of self-control. The successful resolution of this tension without an excess of anger provides the strength of will to choose one's way and to choose God's way later. Without this strength the pastor will become a "people pleaser."

Jesus modeled autonomy in Cana of Galilee when he said to his mother, "My hour has not yet come" (John 2:4). He had begun to model the same strength in Jerusalem when he was twelve. In answer to his mother's query, he said, "I must be about my Father's business" (Luke 2:49, KJV). Though he spent years in Nazareth "subject" to his mother and father, he had also developed the ego strength to be his own person.

Stage Three

The third stage for Erikson is *initiative vs. guilt.* This crisis arises out of the developing power of new mental functions and the ability to move about. Here the little person with a surplus of energy is always moving, going, and doing. In this stage the child develops locomotion. Having mastered the skills of crawling and walking, the child takes the initiative to move away from the mother and explore the world.

In this crisis, the developing person achieves the ability to act independently, to begin activities without an excessive dependence on the authority of another. Great delight comes from planning, attacking, and making a conquest.

To fail in this crisis creates an unhealthy dependence, manifested later in a passive, even hopeless, resignation to fate, sometimes mislabeled as God's will. And the failure to take initiative has the negative consequence of guilt: "I am bad. I have done wrong."

God calls each person to act out of the created power that has been given, and the confidence to initiate arises from this crisis. This action must express the integrity of the person's own being. This does not mean rejecting God's sovereignty, but actualizing the delegated power God has given.

With respect to spiritual development, we do not initiate the relation with God; we respond. God calls us to love our neighbor. The definition of love and its concrete expression must be decided by each person. The energy, forms, and patterns originate in these earliest experiences. The failure to move away, to be expressive, to risk, results in guilt, a mood that may later pervade the relation with God.

Jesus modeled the resolution of this stage when he said, "We must work the works of him who sent me" (John 9:4).

Stage Four

Erikson's fourth stage is *industry vs. inferiority.* This primal struggle comes for the child between ages six and twelve. Parents, teachers, adults, friends provide the setting to make things with others and grow in self-confidence.

The strength or virtue of this stage is confidence, the conviction that one can do or make something that will be valued by others. It arises first from the ability to draw, to write, and to build. This attitude flows over into wider relations and actions, building a confidence in one's competence to do whatever job one is called to do.

This stage enables a person to feel confident about making a contribution to others, to life, to history, about doing something that will be valued by others, particularly by God. However, this feeling of competence may become perverted into the idea of judgment by performance. The heresy of justification by works may begin in this crisis.

On the positive side, God calls the developing person to become a co-creator, a co-laborer with God. If one does not develop a basic sense of competency, one will often reject God's call as Moses sought to do when he asked, "Who am I that I should [do this thing]?" (Ex. 3:11).

Because spirituality refers to the core of one's life, the response we make to God's call affects both attitude and action. This crisis invites a confidence in one's ability to make a contribution in life. The confidence that arises from this struggle lies at the heart of meaning in life—my life and all its

involvements matter to God, and my actions have the capability of glorify-
ing God.

Jesus said, "My Father is working still, and I am working" (John 5:17).
He also said, "For the works which the Father has granted me to accom-
plish, these very works which I am doing, bear me witness that the Father
has sent me" (John 5:36). Jesus had the freedom to affirm his competence
and the value of his work, but with an appropriate humility he recognized
that only through God was he able to do these things.

Stage Five

Erikson's fifth crisis is *identity vs. role confusion.* This crisis comes ini-
tially in adolescence during those years when young people seek an identity.
Characteristically, adolescents try out various roles. They assume them
quickly, test them, and easily dispose of some of them. The greatest influence on their choices is the reaction and response of their peers.

In this stage young people also develop their persona, the face they wear
for the world. The cues for developing this mask come from the responses
of approval and disapproval from peers. In some form, however, the question of identity remains hidden in all the remaining stages. Each new crisis
invites a new and deeper look at one's identity.

A failure to achieve a favorable ratio of identity over diffusion means the
sacrifice of the unique self that one was created to be. Those who fail to
develop an adequate sense of self cling to the persona, an artificial self
designed to please others. This choice or failure results in a generation of
hollow men and women.

Through this crisis, God invites us to recognize our true identity as
children of God. As God's children, we still experience our identity in
myriad forms. All pastors must discover those gifts and possibilities at the
core of their being and risk expressing them. In some respects identity
continues to be the issue for the spiritually maturing person. An encounter
with God in which grace addresses the person creates a new identity: child
of God. In adolescence this identity becomes more potent than in childhood
years. While the identity as God's child carries over into later stages, its
shape and content change. For example, God's call to fill a special office
reopens the identity question. In other stages of life the question of identity
will be considered when the last child leaves home and when retirement
comes. To forget that one is a child of God is, from a spiritual perspective,
role diffusion. The firmness of one's personal identity enhances the clarity
of one's spiritual identity.

Jesus experienced the fullness of his identity at his baptism. As he came
out of the water, the heavens opened and he heard a voice saying, "This is
my beloved Son, with whom I am well pleased" (Matt. 3:17). This identity
was confirmed again by the voice that spoke on the mount of transfigura-

tion, "This is my beloved Son . . . listen to him" (Matt. 17:5). His identity was strengthened by the night of prayer in the garden of Gethsemane; he maintained that confidence in the dark hour on the cross when he cried out, "Into thy hands I commit my spirit!" (Luke 23:46).

Stage Six

Erikson's sixth stage of development is *intimacy vs. isolation.* The primal matrix for the initiation of this stage is engagement, marriage, and sexual union of male and female. Like all the other issues, this one, too, has been present latently in earlier stages and continues to manifest itself in later stages. But in young adulthood this issue moves to the center of the developmental stage.

The possibility of intimacy arises from the development of a firm identity, a knowledge of who one is, what one wants, and the competency to be that person consistently with others. These strengths combine to enable a meaningful, lasting commitment.

All the strengths developed in earlier stages stand behind the invitation to intimacy: a basic trust in the goodness of God and of life; a separate self, capable of making an autonomous decision; a self that can respond to the call of God and have a degree of confidence that a person can do what God wills. These earlier crises and the strengths they call forth provide the developing person strength to surrender to another.

In spiritual development these strengths make possible a conscious, decisive surrender to God. The absence of these strengths does not, to the contrary, mean that persons cannot surrender to God. Failure in the earlier stages will, however, create problems in a relation with God. Often persons have difficulty responding to the grace of God, not because they do not wish to but because they fear a loss of identity in the relation. These persons experience the same fear in closeness to a mate or friend. They are disposed to feel that God has forsaken them or that God is not interested in them. These fears are often the projection upon God of their own failures. In order for such persons to have a mature relation with God, these early failures must be reworked; perhaps they should be valued as invitations to growth.

Recall Peter's promise to follow Jesus and never fall away. To this, Jesus remarked, "Before the cock crows, you will deny me three times" (Matt. 26:34). Peter lacked an autonomous, competent self that could make a decisive commitment to Christ. His inflated ego gave him an exalted opinion of himself. The failure did not mean that Peter was not a friend to Christ, but it indicates that he still had unresolved issues.

To fail in intimacy leads to fear of and resistance to commitment. Without commitment of the self, there can be no intimacy between persons. Isolation, loneliness, and emptiness result, between friends and mates as well as between the soul and God.

In this stage, God acts in the context of our struggle for intimacy, calling us to discipleship—a total commitment of ourselves to him. Without identity, commitment will be fragile and ambiguous; God will often seem distant and unavailable.

In this and succeeding stages, identity will be reworked to express itself in a deeper and deeper relationship with God. The depth of the relation does not destroy a person's individuality and uniqueness; rather, like a finely cut diamond, each person, through intimacy with God, expresses a different reflection of God's love.

The matter of intimacy impinges upon pastoral spirituality in two significant ways. First, the pastor's personal intimacy with God depends on the ability to risk oneself in surrender to God. This risk manifests itself in a response of faith to Christ's initial call. Again, this risk of self demonstrates itself in a response to God's call to a particular office.

Second, this intimacy with God reveals itself in the minister's ability to embrace pastoral roles: symbolic presence, director of the drama of worship, spiritual guide, leader, servant of Christ. Becoming intimate with these roles enables the minister to exemplify more fully the intention of God.

Jesus' identity was tested in the desert. There the enemy said, "If you are the Son of God . . ." (Luke 4:3), and in each temptation Jesus heard the call of God to surrender more fully to God. The dark night in the garden was yet another test, and Jesus responded, "Not my will, but thine, be done" (Luke 22:42). In his darkest hour on the cross he questioned his intimacy with the Father: "My God, my God, why hast thou forsaken me?" (Matt. 27:46). The search for intimacy will always be tested.

Stage Seven

Erikson's seventh stage of *generativity vs. stagnation* arises in the marriage relationship; the creation of children, including their training and care, models the purpose of this stage. For those persons who do not marry, this stage is expressed in friendships and in a commitment to work.

Generativity builds on the competency derived from the industry vs. inferiority crisis (the fourth stage), in which one's worthwhileness is affirmed by what one has made. This earlier strength feeds into the seventh stage, giving the person a sense that what is generated has value.

But it is not only the strength of the fourth stage that is important here. All the previous stages come together: basic trust in the goodness of God, a confidence in oneself, a sense of purpose, a competence in the use of skills, and a self committed to God. In this stage of generativity these strengths find expression in new creations through the Spirit.

The dominant motif of generative spirituality is that of caring. Personal and social creations matter—persons, life, art, culture, history, and institutions. Spirituality expresses itself in creating children of the kingdom, mentoring, stewardship, church renewal, and equipping the church for mission: caring about the things that matter most in this world.

The generative virtue of making and caring for what one has made is seen in Jesus' high priestly prayer (John 17). The disciples have been his major project; he has made them and equipped them to re-present him in the world. He has kept his followers, cared for them to the end, and passed on to them the tasks of preaching and doing God's will in the world.

The minister in this stage has a spirituality of productivity (ages thirty-five to sixty-five, the bulk of life): calling forth new life, nurturing and caring for it, building the congregation with programs and budgets and members, training and developing persons for mission in the world, caring for the institutions—church, school, government, society. In later years the minister must mentor the children of God, to pass on to them the power, responsibility, and skills that have been acquired. But generative spirituality keeps its spiritual grounding in a call to share as a co-laborer in God's work in the world. (Chapters 6 through 10 explore in greater depth how the minister engages with God in this task.)

Stage Eight

Erikson's eighth stage is *integrity vs. despair.* The matrix for the formation of integrity is bounded by retirement and death, as one faces the no-more of being. This setting calls for the reevaluation of a person's one and only life.

Integrity implies that a person has accepted his or her life, with its joys, sorrows, griefs, achievements, successes, and failures, and has resolved life's basic conflicts in a favorable ratio. With most of the course run, the athlete of God stands in the presence of the Most High offering the fulfilled life, the mature love, and the loving devotion that rightfully belongs to God now and forever!

Destiny, inherent in each stage, receives the spotlight in the last stage. Either individuals have fulfilled their destiny by this time, or they have not. The despair of this stage arises when one sees what might have been and realizes that it is too late now to attempt it. The threat of despair must surely hasten the decision to be who we are created to be.

One who has not attained the final stage of life can write about it only with anticipation. Those of us who have not reached that period should be given the right to revise when informed by experience. This final stage represents the fruition of a whole life in which one affirms that the struggle and pain have been worth the result, or one confesses in despair or resignation that no meaning has been found. Somewhere before we reach this final stage, we need to find a place to reflect on our past, to be guided in the investment of life to the glory of God. Doubtless that desire comes to many in their mid-fifties, in anticipation of retirement, old age, and death. The influence of the end of life gives a sense of urgency and value to the present by pointing toward this final stage.

In the stage of integrity, Jesus heard the call of God and was able to say, "Not my will, but thine, be done." And in the final moment of his life, to say, "Into your hands I commit my spirit." And, finally, "It is finished" (John 19:30).

Development and Tom MacGreggor

If we wear the lenses of this developmental theory and view the life of Tom MacGreggor, what do we discover about his formation, call, and spiritual dynamics? If we ask Tom when he became a Christian, he will probably be unable to give us a date. His journey began in a small town where he went to Sunday school and church. From his earliest years his mind was filled with pictures of Jesus, and he was told repeatedly about the love of God. The Bible stories furnished him models, though he gave them little conscious consideration.

When Tom was nine, he had periods of mood change. Sometimes he felt depressed and viewed the world as a scary place. He often wondered what would happen to him if his mother died or left him. These feelings combined to cause him the pain of insecurity. These formative experiences cannot be divorced from his question about God and his relation to God. Perhaps the burnout at thirty-eight had roots in these early experiences.

At age eleven a neighbor's car ran over Corky, his cat. The cat's death gave him his first awareness that he too would die. When he spoke with his mother about this concern, she told him about the death and resurrection of Jesus. Yet this question awakened Tom to his own finitude, an awareness that stayed with him. The awakening of his consciousness to death came at about the time he began attending confirmation class. Along with a number of his friends he was confirmed at age twelve.

At age fifteen Tom attended a church camp. On the closing evening the campers gathered around a bonfire, wrote their sins on pieces of paper, and tossed them into the flames. This experience was very important to Tom. He came back from camp feeling close to God. In those adolescent years he saw in Jesus a model, a hero to follow and imitate. His participation in the Fellowship of Christian Athletes supported this decision. During his fifteenth and sixteenth years he considered the ministry several times. All these experiences fit neatly into Erikson's stage five, identity vs. role confusion.

During college Tom bailed out on his religious development. He was a Pi Kappa Alpha, and the Pikas weren't known for Christian piety or serious study. He met and fell in love with Margie on a memorable football weekend. Choosing real estate as a vocation, he got a good job after graduation and in four years opened his own office. At this point Tom and Margie returned to the church. Margie was pregnant with their first child. Tom was dealing with intimacy vs. isolation and the beginning of generativity.

When he was twenty-eight, he attended a lay retreat for churchmen. On this retreat he was confronted with a deeper call from Christ. The leader said in the closing service, "God can take an ordinary person and do extra-ordinary things with him, if he surrenders himself completely to God." At the close of the service Tom made a serious surrender of himself. At that time the idea of the ministry returned. He struggled with his discomfort for a long time before he told Margie.

At age twenty-eight Tom had entered the generative stage fully. He had a child, a business, and a life before him. He felt the pressure to find meaning. Would the real estate business give him the sense of meaning that ministry in the church would? Did God want his life spent in the business world or in the church? These questions arose in part from the stage in which Tom found himself, but they also presented themselves through the gospel message and the Spirit of God. At the beginning of the generative stage Tom felt concern about what he could give his life to, a concern all persons in this stage share. As a Christian and as one who had previously considered ordained ministry, Tom found in this stage the context he needed to reconsider the ministry. The stage provided the formal aspect of commitment; the gospel message offered the material aspect, the content. In making a commitment to enter the ministry, Tom reworked his intimacy with Christ; a better formed identity enabled him to make a deeper commitment of himself and to consider the ministry as a vocation.

We began to engage Tom at age thirty-eight, ten years after his decision to enter the ministry. The emptiness and lack of reality he expressed regarding the ministry indicated the unfavorable ratio of stagnation to generativity in his life. In part this personal crisis may also have been triggered by the lack of successful resolution of issues that arose in earlier stages of growth. Though Tom achieved a favorable ratio of basic trust vs. mistrust in his earliest stage, he still experiences elements of mistrust that distress him. His anxiety and resulting depression as a child indicate that he may have work yet to do. Perhaps, too, his lack of a favorable resolution regarding autonomy lies beneath his compulsiveness.

The energy consumed by these unresolved crises leads to personal and vocational burnout. No amount of resolve and increase of activity can heal the situation. Realizing this fact, Tom MacGreggor has turned to the original source of energy, the call of God. Yet he still must deal with the failed crises that affect the hearing of God's call.

Stages and Spirituality

Suppose we could listen to Tom MacGreggor's thoughts after he had completed a reflection on the crises of his life. What has he learned about the relation of his personal development to his spirituality? First, he has discovered that life is a dynamic process of hearing and responding to God's call at different times in his life.

Tom has recognized that he must maintain an openness to changing forms of his experience with God. The ways that God has come to him in the past are not necessarily the ways God will come in the future. The novel ways of God suggest new ways of prayer, new forms of obedience, different types of worship.

Spirituality, Tom has begun to discover, is a dynamic union of the natural and the spiritual. He is a real human being; God is a real God. Who he is as a person cannot be denied or ignored in this relation: failed crises as well as acquired strengths both have their influence; different stages offer different vistas through which to perceive God. God's reality is communicated in a thousand different ways, often in novelty.

Since God is always calling, Tom has realized that he must keep listening for the call. Whatever else it may be, spirituality is a personal response to the God who calls and calls and calls. . . .

After Tom finished reflecting intensely on his life, he had a profound conviction that God had been calling him through each of the stages. One evening not long afterward, he was in the basement working on a plaque when Margie stuck her head in the door.

"What are you making?"

"A plaque to hang on my study wall," Tom responded.

"What does it say?" she asked.

Tom held it up so she could see.

ALWAYS ON THE ROAD
AND
UNDER CANVAS

5 Toward a Pastoral Piety

The retreat leader passed out a blue sheet entitled A PRAYER INVENTORY. Tom read the list.

1. How much time do I spend daily in a disciplined experience of prayer?

2. What methods have I discovered for reading the Bible in a way that the scriptures nurture my experience of God?

3. Do I have one or more spiritual companions who share the journey with me and to whom I am accountable?

4. Has there been a time in my life that God seemed nearer than today?

5. To what extent is prayer integrated into my life?

6. Do I seek times of solitude in which I am alone with God? How often?

7. What other sources of spiritual nurture do I have?

8. When was the last time I made a spiritual retreat?

9. Is my consciousness of God related to the issues facing the world?

10. What in my life rivals God for priority?

As he read the last question, Tom heard the retreat leader saying, "These are the questions I ask myself to check up on my devotion to God."

Tom had some negative feelings about the whole enterprise of setting up disciplines for himself; he knew too many pious persons, proud of the time they spent in prayer, who appeared to him as "goody-goody," and he wanted none of that earnest pretense. His bitter experience with Jim Councilman had been enough to frighten him away from this type of routine.

Yet, Tom argued with himself, surely, there was a way of meeting God that would result in a genuine life of devotion, one free of the religiosity I deplore.

The second day of the retreat Tom arranged to eat lunch with Marian

Black, the retreat leader for this particular group of twelve ministers. During the meal he told Marian that for several months his life had taken a turn toward God. He related the events of the night the phone call came from Jesse Van Meeter, his subsequent visits with him, and the difficulty he was having with a consistent time of prayer.

"I've tried reading the Bible and having daily prayer, but it just doesn't work for me. My mind wanders to a thousand other things, nothing happens in me, and I find it easy to neglect the time."

"Your prayer is only prayer if it enables you to do what God wills, to love," Marian suggested.

"I don't see anything happening," Tom complained.

Marian offered him wisdom he was unprepared to receive. "Prayer is like a blanket," she explained. "A blanket is only a blanket if it keeps you warm; prayer is only prayer if it brings you into a relation with God.

"But," Marian continued, "be slow to judge that it has no effect on you. More may be happening than you realize; not all transformation is conscious."

"I never thought about that," Tom told her. "But I still need help in being consistent in my time with God."

"Tom," Marian said, "one of my mentors in spiritual growth says, 'Discipline is absolutely central to the development of any kind of skill, whether it is in sports, in scientific discovery, or in learning to love or pray.' "[1]

"I suppose I'm looking for an easy way that doesn't require too much."

Marian explained further. "A disciple must be disciplined. To be disciplined means to get control of your actions so that you are not pushed around either by your unconscious or by other persons."

"What sort of program do you recommend?" Tom asked with interest.

Marian looked thoughtful for a few moments. "I have a hunch that if I gave you a formula for prayer, it would be more a deterrent than a help. Instead, let me tell you a story.

"Last month, when I met with my spiritual companion, she set a bottle of wine on the table and said nothing. I picked up the bottle, read the label, lifted the cork, even sniffed the bouquet. Then I set it down again.

"My guide said, 'You have examined all the outward characteristics of the wine, but one thing is missing—wine is for drinking!' Prayer is like that."

Marian waited for the point to sink in. Finally, she broke the silence. "As a retreat leader I don't want to be like the old saint who spoke on prayer, directed his listeners in the ways of prayer, and urged them to pray. And all the listeners followed his lead. They too spoke on prayer, taught the ways of prayer, and urged others to pray. But nobody prayed."

Tom left the table deep in thought. He made his way out to the lake and sat on the bank a long time, just thinking. How do I find a piety that works for me? he wondered. The question stayed with him through the remaining hours of the two-day retreat.

In the closing worship, Tom thought back on the forty-eight hours and tried to summarize its value. During this time he had been free of the demands of the parish; he had spent time in silence; God had seemed near; he had shared his story with other struggling ministers; he felt the challenge to be more disciplined in his life with God.

Marian, whom he had come to respect as a spiritual guide, was speaking. "Mary has chosen the better part. . . . This story of Jesus is about priorities. . . . What is important to you? What will you put first in your life?"

On the way home Tom kept asking himself, "What is important to me?" He discerned in himself a growing interest in God; God was of primary importance, and he resolved to search for a piety that nurtured his concern. During the retreat Marian had talked about types of spirituality. In the lecture she offered seven styles. Tom wrote to Marian requesting a copy of this lecture. He read and reread it, underlining those characteristics that seemed appropriate for him. Through this process he began to sort out his new learnings about piety. Here is a copy of Marian's lecture on types of spirituality. (See Figure 4.)

Types of Spirituality

In the long history of the church, devotion to God has taken various forms. We will explore these forms of piety, and our analysis will be guided by six definitive questions. Where is this form of piety to be found—what is its setting? How is God mediated to human consciousness? How does this form of piety manifest itself in personal experience? What practices reinforce it? What type of personality would find it appropriate?* What are its strengths and weaknesses? We will ask these questions of evangelical piety, charismatic piety, sacramental piety, activist piety, academic piety, ascetic piety, and Eastern piety.

EVANGELICAL PIETY is a form of spirituality found in conservative churches with a puritan or revivalist tradition. In evangelical piety, persons encounter God through the word of God. By reading the scriptures, understanding the authoritative message, discerning the will of God, and doing the will of God, persons experience true and vital spirituality.

Normally this type of piety expresses itself in personal witness to others, using speech punctuated with references to God or the Holy Spirit, with an aim toward conversion or edification of the hearer. Generally, this approach to God provides clear guidelines for living the Christian life.

This piety develops in the closet: that is, it grows through a daily discipline of time set aside for prayer and reading the Bible. It includes meditation on the scriptures, fasting, and days of prayer.

---

*See Figure 2 and the discussion in chapter 3.

Evangelical piety has a strong appeal to the sensate, extroverted type of personality. Such persons find reading the scriptures, prayer, and witnessing to fit their temperament. They also like to have things spelled out in black and white.

The strengths of this style come from its intentionality to build on the biblical revelation. It creates a passionate people, willing to work and sacrifice their lives for Jesus Christ. The commitment to make God's will a priority is admirable. Personal devotion to Christ, sacrifice of self, and sacrifice of personal resources are authentic expressions of Christian discipleship.

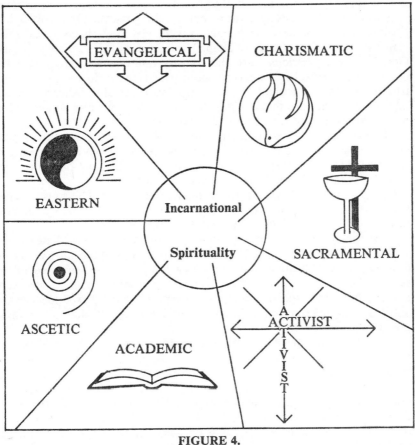

FIGURE 4.
Types of spirituality.

The weaknesses of evangelical piety stem from its tendency toward legalism, which breeds a judgmental spirit. Sometimes the form of spirituality remains after the life of the Spirit has gone out of it.

CHARISMATIC PIETY has a kinship with evangelical piety in the seriousness of its devotion. Found primarily in Pentecostal, neo-Pentecostal, and nondenominational congregations, it is also scattered throughout mainline denominations, especially in Episcopal and Roman Catholic churches and, in a lesser degree, Methodist and Presbyterian churches. Charismatic spirituality is associated with the gift of the Holy Spirit and the Spirit's present activity in the body of Christ. God is experienced in the immediate presence of the Spirit. The Bible mediates this experience, but the experience also is drawn from study and sharing groups, praise services, and charismatic worship.

Charismatic piety expresses itself in the charismatic group or congregation through a demonstration of the gifts of the Spirit. Some groups demand that believers speak in tongues as an evidence of possessing the Holy Spirit. Charismatics often have an insider way of speaking that sets off their identity: "Praise the Lord"; "Thank you, Jesus"; "Hallelujah"; "Praise God." These expressions mark the conversation of many newly initiated charismatics. Each charismatic community tends to develop its own specialized vocabulary. Charismatics, like evangelicals, are also dedicated to witnessing. Not only are they seeking to win the lost but also to evangelize other Christians into the charismatic experience.

The charismatic also studies the word of God and prays. In private devotions, the devotee may use a prayer language known as "speaking in tongues." This form of spirituality finds support in a group or community that shares the experience and practices the gifts.

Charismatic piety appeals to the intuitive, feeling type. These persons feel the depths of their devotion to Christ. Most will tend to be extroverted rather than introverted in a demonstration of the gifts.

The strength of charismatic spirituality is found in the immediate experience of God. Those in the fellowship who have been touched by God also have a depth of dedication, making them willing to risk and sacrifice for the sake of the gospel of Christ. This spirituality usually reaches across economic, educational, social, and racial barriers. The shared experience of the Spirit and a supernatural worldview provide a center that binds these diverse persons together.

The weaknesses in charismatic spirituality stem from its emphasis on intuition, feeling, and experience, often to the neglect of intellectual substance and form. Like other kinds of spirituality, there may also be imitations of the true gift of the Spirit. Frequently, this spirituality is otherworldly, with little concern for social transformation. In the worst case, charismatic spirituality lacks a deep self-awareness and covers ignorance with religious experience and enthusiasm. In this latter form, the charismatic experience can hide personality deficiencies and defend against painful growth.

SACRAMENTAL PIETY, standing in contrast to charismatic piety though it may become compatible with it, is found predominantly among Roman Catholics, Greek Orthodox, and Episcopalians. The presence of God in sacramental piety is mediated through the sacraments and the liturgy. In eating the bread and drinking the wine, the worshiper encounters the real presence. Liturgical prayers and the celebrations of the church year offer additional channels of God's Spirit.

Sacramental piety expresses itself in a sacramental life. The liturgy of worship, the church year, festivals, and celebrations provide the structure of sacramental piety. The world of nature, viewed sacramentally, also mediates the presence of God. History contributes to sacramental piety as the unfolding of God's story.

Worship offers the setting for strengthening sacramental spirituality, especially public worship. It is further strengthened through the prayer book, private bidding prayer, and spiritual reading.

Sacramental spirituality appeals to the sensate, thinking type. This spirituality has a "thereness" about it that gives it objectivity even when feelings dry up. The liturgy offers a structure and also creates space for thought and reflection.

The strength of this form of spirituality is its objectivity, especially in the sacraments. The sacraments are valid despite the inauthenticity or lack of awareness within the worshiper. This spirituality orders life and gives stability to it in the face of the abyss of nonbeing. A sacramental view of nature and history gives a certain "at homeness" to life in the world.

One of the dangers of sacramental spirituality is a dependence upon ritual that can become empty. When the liturgy dies, worshipers leave the sanctuary empty and hollow. This form of spirituality often fails to emphasize personal disciplines and radical discipleship. It tends to favor corporate spiritual formation over personal spiritual formation.

ACTIVIST PIETY is found predominantly in the left wing of mainline denominations and in religious issue-oriented groups like the peace, feminist, gay, and ecology movements.

The activist meets God not primarily in the church or in religious practices but in social service and political action. God is already at work in the world, and the activist meets the Holy One by joining in that divine Providence in the world. The historical arena provides the setting for a meeting with the living God; the Eternal Mystery is not buried in a dead past but is present *now,* transforming history.

An activist piety expresses itself in action. It aims to function in solidarity with God in specific social transformations. This form of devotion contrasts markedly with a private, cloistered, passive piety.

The activist finds renewed energy and motivation from grasping a new issue, serving on a task force, challenging the establishment, protesting the status quo. The activist also draws strength from others involved in the mission.

An activist piety appeals to an extroverted, intuitive, feeling type. These persons intend to make a difference in the world. They feel deeply about causes and possess high ideals. Even though they may fail to reach their noble goals, they are willing to sacrifice both themselves and their resources in an effort to change the present order of life. Change is a dominant motif of the activists.

Perhaps the weakness of this approach, as commendable as it may be, comes from its lack of spiritual depth. Activists sometimes lose the awareness of God in the action that purports to be a manifestation of the will of God. When this occurs, action degenerates into works righteousness and human effort. Disillusionment follows. Cynicism is the ripened fruit of disillusionment. When burnout comes, the once brave, vigorous disciples find themselves paralyzed. The value of this approach is its relevance and ethical commitment. An activist piety aims to change the real world. It is an idealistic piety that defines spirituality in terms of the kingdom of God and gives concrete expression to a vision of transformation.

ACADEMIC PIETY is quite the opposite of activist piety. To some persons, academics and piety present contradictory images. In the popular mind, piety appeals to feeling rather than intellect. But those persons who think about God and systematize their thought express their relationship with God through the mind. Probably the most outstanding example is Thomas Aquinas, who wrote the *Summa Theologica* and in the end was given a beatific vision of God.

This piety, which consists of research and thoughtful reflection, is found in scholars, theologians, teachers, and studious clergy.

The encounter with God for the academicians is mediated through rational thought. Their research results in a system that relates the truth of God to life; their deep awareness of God comes through reason. They love God with their whole mind.

This kind of spirituality expresses itself in a lifestyle of study, careful analysis of issues, reflection, and teaching. When the system is completed, the academic feels fulfilled.

This piety finds strength and reinforcement in the professional academy. Academics express themselves in reading, studious reflection, occasional papers, discussion of insights with a discerning mind, and writing books.

Academic piety has the strongest appeal to an introverted, intuitive, thinking type. These persons tackle complex issues and seek to know and understand reality. They are less concerned with sharing their insights with others than are the extroverted types.

The weaknesses of academic piety may be found in its frequent loss of a reverence for the Holy; the approach can focus on the data of theology or the specific issues that are being addressed, rather than the One behind the data. It can become cold and impersonal. The scholar may have an answer, but may also have little passion for involvement in life. This form of spirituality, though valuable, sometimes ends in cynicism.

Academic spirituality shows strength in its ruthless pursuit of truth; it faces the issues of life boldly and honestly. This spirituality moves in new directions as the truth demands. It resists both a weak sentimentalism and a shallow, superficial emotionalism.

ASCETIC PIETY is found among priests and nuns in religious orders. In its Protestant form it appears in world-denying holiness movements. Some lay persons may also be ascetic in discipline and practice. Ignatius, for example, formed the third order for laity who were married and engaged in the practical affairs of life but lived out the monastic ideal in the world.

For the ascetic, God is met daily in the divine office, spiritual literature, and mental prayer. The ascetic lives a life of contemplation and self-denial as an expression of devotion to God.

The lifestyle of the ascetic who lives in a cloistered society centers around prayer, rest, and work. Simplicity is the key to the ascetic life, which is reinforced by the threefold vow of poverty, chastity, and obedience.

This type of piety will appeal to introverted, sensate types. Their introversion enables them to endure the silence and solitude, while their sensate abilities orient them to the facts of the outer world.

There are some dangers in the ascetic approach. It can become an escape from the world, though it need not. It requires a rigid discipline that denies human hungers. This formal discipline can also become a routine that loses its meaning. Monastics are not exempt from emptiness or dryness of soul.

This style has a clear, corporate discipline that orders life and gives it support. In its best form, it is an unselfish offering of one's life in prayer for the world. It demands a life of simplicity and studied concentration on God.

EASTERN PIETY is found in Buddhism, often in groups of monks who seek union with God. In this approach the seeker usually pictures God as part of the self; to get in touch with the self is to get in touch with God. Transcendence is within the person.

The religious experience of the East manifests itself in inward peace, often resulting in a withdrawal from the world; its goal is the loss of the self and the cessation of desire.

This experience can be strengthened by a disciplined practice of meditation, fasting, and solitude. Though meditation may be a group practice, it tends toward a strong individualism.

Persons who are introverted, feeling types will find this approach most compatible with their temperament. Other persons with thinking as a dominant function may achieve this union with the All but with greater effort.

The strength of this type of piety lies in its demand for control over the body and its appetites; it offers welcome relief from active engagement for rushed souls. From a Christian perspective its weakness comes from a lack of interest in history, in the welfare of individual persons, and in passionate involvement in the world. And, of course, the Eastern approach lacks a center in Jesus Christ. For a Christian, Christ is the source, the norm, and the goal of spirituality.

After Tom had finished reviewing Marian's lecture, he was confronted with the task of shaping his own spirituality. What type or types of piety would inform his practice?

Actually, he didn't like the word "piety" because it reminded him of Jim

Councilman and a whole class of persons from whom he wished to dissociate himself. These rejected models made a great demonstration of their religious devotion but often seemed lacking in human respect, to say nothing of Christian love.

Tom recalled Marian's definition of piety. She said that piety has a deeper meaning and comes from the Latin *pietas,* which means "devotion to religious duties and practices." Piety referred to a particular form of devotion to God. If this was the meaning of piety, Tom could see no reason why pastoral piety should not be a matter of immediate concern. He concluded that pastoral piety meant the deepening of one's faith through an encounter with God and expressing the experience of the divine presence in creative ministry. This meeting with God would take a form, however. What form should his devotion to God take? Satisfied with his new definition, Tom was now ready to formulate his style of piety, one constructed, he believed, from the best of the seven styles Marian had identified.

Toward a Pastoral Piety

As Tom reflected on his learnings from the retreat, he made a tentative outline of the kind of piety that seemed to possess integrity and to be adequate and appropriate for him. Perhaps his piety could be identified as incarnational, drawing upon each of the other types and combining them into a new creative whole. He made the following entry in his journal:

My piety must be connected to the church, the body of Christ, a community of worship. I cannot abide the individualism of the East or the perverted individualism of evangelical piety. While the main setting will be in the corporate community, I recognize the importance of scheduled times alone for private worship.

I believe that God comes to me through the external events of history and nature, human intelligence, theology, the Bible, and the Christian tradition. The presence of God also comes to consciousness through the inner world of intuition and imagination.

My piety must express itself in a simplified, Christ-centered life of love. I see the need to withdraw from activity to be renewed by the Spirit. But I will also meet God as I serve others. I believe that my life can be enriched through periods of silence during which time I keep open to the inner depths of the Spirit. I must listen for the word of God in the silence as it relates to the world of action.

I believe this form of piety will be reinforced through personal and corporate worship and through a daily time for meditation on scripture or some other spiritual writing. Regular retreats, plus partaking of the Eucharist, will enrich my sense of the Presence. I will also find strength in sharing with a spiritual companion.

I believe that my piety must search for a balance between extroversion and introversion, sensation and intuition, thinking and feeling. I will grow as I explore those sides of my functioning with which I am least competent.

The piety I have set forth for myself recognizes the importance of the biblical norms of an evangelical piety, the freedom of the Spirit to grasp human consciousness immediately as in charismatic piety, the sacramental nature of life and the ordering of life in a sacred way from sacramental piety, the necessity for engagement with real needs and the issues of persons as found in activist piety, the importance of developing the intellect as emphasized by the academics, and the need for periodic retreat for personal denial and self-examination as demonstrated by the monastics. This style of spirituality seems holistic, balanced, corporate, and personal.

After Tom had put together an eclectic piety that had both relevance and integrity, he reread his journal entry. Everything in his soul affirmed what he had written, but he also knew that this intellectual enterprise stood at a distance from a disciplined practice of devotion. His best intentions would remain an ideal for his life without a regular time with God in which he honestly faced his betrayals of these noble desires.

As Tom reflected on his devotional ideal, he knew also that this form of spirituality was vulnerable to the same perversions that he reacted against. His emphasis on biblical authority and Christ as the norm of spirituality could degenerate into reading the Bible from duty or creating his own brand of religious legalism, as Jim Councilman had done. He also realized that in searching for personal experience, he could make experience into an idol, a mistake he had noted in some charismatics. All the liabilities of other forms of spirituality lay before him as traps to be avoided. Like every other human being, he as a minister had to struggle for balance, integrity, and authenticity. Nothing in the spiritual life is automatic, except temptation.

Tom looked through his notes and found one of Marian's handouts. He used it as a guide to examine his spiritual discipline.

An Examination of Pastoral Piety

Use the following questions to examine your life of devotion. Your answers will enable you to look at your practice of piety clearly and honestly.

What is the meaning of piety to you?

In what setting do you most often experience the presence of God?

What has been your history regarding piety?

What kind of piety was expressed in your religious community of origin?

How did seminary training affect your view of piety?

What is your present practice of piety?

How is the awareness of God mediated to you? How often are you consciously in the presence of God? What seems to make God's presence more real for you?

How does your piety manifest itself in specific behavior?

What seems to deepen or revitalize your piety?

What is the relationship of your piety to your personality type? Are you introverted or extroverted? Are you sensate or intuitive? Are you thinking or feeling? Do you see how your preferences shape your approach to spirituality?

What strengths of your present piety do you wish to preserve and deepen?

What changes do you need to make in order to have a more adequate spirituality?

Answering these questions in his journal, coupled with his new understanding of piety, set Tom on a firm path toward a new spiritual plane in his life.

6 The Pastor as a Christ-Bearer

Since that Saturday night over a year ago when his friend Jesse called, Tom had begun to change a great deal in his life and ministry. In fact, he had experienced a renewal of faith and vision.

As he sat in Jesse's office, he reviewed aloud the changes he had gone through. When he finished, his spiritual companion sat there with his eyes closed for a full five minutes. Tom was getting accustomed to this. He had decided that in the silence his guide was listening for God in the things he heard Tom say.

Finally, Jesse spoke. "How will you relate your new sense of call and your deepened awareness of God to your ministry?"

"I can already see a difference," Tom responded. "My preparation for preaching is easier. I am speaking with a greater freedom, and the dull professionalism I felt a year ago has begun to dissolve."

"Good, good." The older minister was nodding his head in approval and celebration. "I think you'll find a continuing source of strength in an understanding of yourself as a bearer of Christ."

"A bearer of Christ!" Tom repeated the words.

"Yes. As one called by God, you have a special role. Not a holier or more powerful one, or one of more privilege, but a role as a bearer of Christ, a symbolic presence of God."

The notion both frightened and challenged Tom MacGreggor.

"Did you ever hear the legend of St. Christopher?"

"Yes," Tom said, as his mind turned back to vacation Bible school days. The summer following the fifth grade, his teacher had told the story of this giant of a man who wanted to serve the strongest master in the world. (There are various versions of the legend of St. Christopher, but this is the one Tom remembered.)

Christopher served a mighty king, but one day the king made the sign of the cross, which, he explained, would ward off the devil. So Christopher sought to join the devil, for obviously he was stronger than the king. While searching for the devil, he encountered the Terrible Knight, who confessed that he was, indeed, the devil. One day as they journeyed together, the Terrible Knight veered away from a cross that stood in his way. When Christopher asked why, the devil told him about a man who was killed on that cross. With that evidence of the devil's fears, Christopher went in search of the Christ, who must be even mightier.

At last he found a hermit who taught him about Jesus. As the hermit finished his instruction, he told Christopher that he must fast if he wished to see Christ. "But I cannot fast because I am such a big man; can you not ask something else of me?"

Then the hermit told him that he must pray if he wished to see Christ. "But I cannot pray long hours; ask something else," Christopher replied.

Finally the old hermit said, "You must live by the river; carry across anyone in need. One day, perhaps, our Lord Christ will show himself to you."

So he carried rich and poor, old and young alike across the river. One day as he slept in his hut, he heard the voice of a child. "Christopher, Christopher, carry me across the river."

Christopher rose, took the child on his back, and began fording the river. As the water rushed by him, he had never before felt so burdened by his load. With the far bank in sight, he summoned all his strength, reached the other side, and gently placed the child on the ground.

"I have never had so much difficulty crossing the river," Christopher said. "I felt as though I had the weight of the world on my shoulders."

The child spoke. "Indeed, you did. I am Jesus, the Christ whom you serve!"

"And, that is what it means to be a Christopher, a Christ-bearer," Tom's Bible school teacher had said.

"To embrace your role as a Christ-bearer is perhaps the most difficult and the most urgent task of one called by God," Jesse was saying. "A Christ-bearer's life becomes an incarnation of Christ, a bearer of the presence of God." That, indeed, was a tall order.

On the way to the hospital to visit a member of the church, Tom felt his mind still whirling with the thought: "Me, a bearer of Christ!" As he felt the weight of this symbolic role, he recalled a visit to one of the members the week before.

He had knocked on the door; a five-year-old answered, saw Tom, and ran to the kitchen calling to his mother. "Mom, Mom! God is at the door!"

"Who?" she inquired with a note of shock.

"God. You know, the man at church who wears the black dress."

Tom hadn't thought much about it at the time, but perhaps he was an image of the sacred in ways he did not understand. "Christ-bearer; image of God; symbol of the sacred." Tom kept repeating these ideas to himself as he parked and made his way to the hospital elevator. He thought about all the tasks of ministry—preaching, teaching, counseling, baptizing, conducting funerals, offering the sacrament of the Lord's Supper—could he, in all these functions of ministry, be the bearer of Christ?

Perhaps more pressing, could he be a bearer of Christ to Juanita Jones in room 803, who had learned yesterday that she had an inoperable malignancy?

Tom MacGreggor has been confronted with an issue with which he must come to grips, a calling to re-present Jesus Christ in his life and ministry. This commission to be a Christ-bearer has its source in the heart of the gospel—created in the image of God, re-created by Christ, called by God to be a servant in the church. These roots of pastoral spirituality must ripen into the fruits of Christian ministry.

The symbolic role of the minister as a Christ-bearer introduces a transition from the *being* of the pastor to the pastor's *doing.* Spirituality includes awareness but extends beyond awareness to a lifestyle and a particular form of ministry. At this point we must ask, "How does the spirituality of being a minister express itself in doing ministry?" When a minister claims to be called of God, to be a set-apart person who represents the will of God in Christ, how does this identity affect the practice of ministry?

The pastor as the image of Christ provides an appropriate transition from being to doing because when the minister is the image of the Sacred, the being *is* the doing. The being of the minister in the image of God is doing ministry. This form of being cannot be created or enhanced by the minister's own efforts. It is gift; it is inherent in the fact of the call. Just like a sacrament, the meaning is experienced in the action.

Understanding the minister as the embodiment of the presence of Christ shifts the focus from the minister as an entertainer, therapist, or manager to an orderer of time, a spiritual guide, a leader who seeks to actualize the will of God in concrete actions. This identification centers the minister in Jesus Christ, as one who has been called by God. This designation does not in any way discount the importance of sermons, management, counseling, or social engagement; rather, this perspective grounds these aspects of ministry in the re-presentation of Christ.

Because we take this role to be crucial for the spirituality of the minister, we will examine the Christ-bearer as symbol, we will see how this symbolic presence is reflected in the self-understanding of the apostle Paul, and we will suggest a responsible stewardship of this unique call.

A Symbolic Role

Pastors are bearers of Christ in all their roles. When Tom's spiritual guide introduced him to the idea that he was a Christ-bearer, he was, of course, speaking symbolically. Tom's encounter with the youngster at the door showed him how the minister of God is perceived symbolically. The story of St. Christopher must not be taken literally; ministers do not carry Christ on their backs or in their arms. But because ministers do claim to be called by Christ, because they profess to speak for God and act for God with respect to holy things, they are identified with the sacred.

When we speak of the minister as Christ-bearer or the image of Christ, we enter the slippery world of symbols. What do we mean by a symbol? How does the symbol function? How is the minister a symbol of Christ? These are the questions Tom MacGreggor must answer if he is to fulfill this role with sensitivity and integrity.

The Nature of Symbol

First, a symbol is multidimensional and therefore gives off different sensations. A symbol is visual; it can be seen and described. A symbol can be felt; it can be experienced through touch. But a symbol is not exhausted by its sensuous character. Take Holy Communion, for example. The bread of communion is white and the wine is red and the taste can be flat or salty. Both have an aroma; the bread can feel rough or smooth. These are the multidimensional aspects of the elements. Communion is not flat; it speaks to different sides of human perception.

In the same way the minister as symbol offers different sensations to persons. Through the minister's presence one receives different sensations —sight, feelings, sounds. All these aspects of the minister's physical presence have the capacity to reveal Christ. The Christ who is no longer present in the flesh can be seen, touched, and heard through the men and women who re-present him.

At the end of a children's sermon in which the minister had told them that Jesus invites them to come to him, a five-year-old, finger pointing upward, asked perceptively, "How does he, way up there, invite us who are way down here?"

"Through ministers like me," the pastor responded. "And through all these people sitting here in the church."

A symbol is not exhausted by its sensuous aspects; symbols point beyond themselves. Look again at the bread and wine. In the consecrated communion the bread and wine mean more than sensuous, tasty elements that give off an aroma; they are more than food and drink for the body. These elements point to "something" beyond their natural being. Without the minister's saying a word, the bread and the wine sitting on a consecrated table point to an upper room, a cross, suffering, death, and resurrection. These particular elements have been drawn into the narrative of Christ's life and death; they point to him and mediate his presence to communities of believers.

The minister as symbol points beyond self to Christ. Tom MacGreggor, for example, by the call of Christ and his consecration to ministry has been drawn into the story of Jesus Christ much like the bread and the wine. By association, his person becomes symbolic. He follows in a long line of persons who have been bearers of Christ. Through his role as a minister, he points beyond himself to Christ. The re-presentation, like the bread and wine, does not depend on the action of the minister; the pointing action is inherent in the role.

A symbol contains more than can be expressed in words. A symbol by nature points to a meaning that transcends rational thought. If words could capture the whole truth, there would be no need for symbols; rational, logical, propositional statements would be adequate. With respect to faith, the bread and the wine speak of the death and life of Christ; but they speak of more than a man on a cross dying. The partaking of these elements points to participation in God's grace, an inclusion that cannot be reduced to words. The elements open the way for persons to participate in the reality toward which the symbols point.

For example, when Tom MacGreggor enters the hospital room of Juanita Jones, who has learned that she has an inoperable cancer, Juanita cannot put into words what she feels and experiences as her pastor stands beside her bed. She knows him as a man; she knows him as a friend; she can identify his imperfections. But when Tom looks into her eyes and holds her hand, he is the bearer of Christ; in that moment he represents more than either of them can put into words.

Symbols cannot be created at will. They are born in historical moments. They may be initiated by a person, but symbols exert power only when they are received and perpetuated by a community. Christ in the upper room took bread, and when he blessed it, he broke it; after supper he took the cup, gave thanks, and gave it to all who sat at the table. The meaning of these simple acts, accompanied with the words "This is my body," "This is my blood," grew out of his impending death. His act created the symbol. There might have been other ways of recalling his death, but none have the impact of the bread and the wine. These simple acts of blessing, breaking, and drinking were received by a community of persons who perpetuated these acts and the meaning they suggested.

The symbolic role of the minister also has its source in that historical moment when Jesus said to Peter and Andrew, "Follow me, and I will make you fishers of men" (Matt. 4:19). This original call, plus the ordination of his apostles (John 20:21–23), forms the primitive ground of the ministerial calling. Christ created the "called ones" just as he created the symbolic bread and wine. We do not create this role for ourselves; it has been created by Christ and fulfilled by all those ministers of his who have preceded us. By answering the call of Christ, Tom placed himself in that long line of called persons. As each new loaf and cup point to Christ, so each new minister called by Christ bears his presence.

The symbol does not exert an effort to transmit its meaning. The symbol "is." A symbol has a quality of "thereness"; the bread and the wine do not do anything as they lie on the communion table; their presence has an inherent power for those who can "see." Trying to make the bread and the wine into the body and blood would violate their symbolic role. What on this earth could claim this high and holy place? The Christian symbol is created by grace or it doesn't exist.

If Tom MacGreggor tries to force the Holy One to use him, to manifest the divine presence through him, he will violate his calling. When he walks into room 803, it is God who chooses to be manifested through Tom. Not only here but in each of the functions of ministry, it is not for Tom to make an effort to impress upon others that he is the bearer of Christ. His efforts will violate the integrity of the symbol.

Finally, a symbol can be broken. The meaning of a particular symbol may cease or be drastically altered. When a symbol is broken, it no longer grasps those who previously have shared its meaning; it no longer points beyond itself but becomes opaque so that the meaning is blocked. When the bread and the wine no longer enable the worshiper to participate in the death and resurrection of Christ, these elements as symbols have been broken. The broken symbol occurs when the person or the community ceases to believe in the reality toward which the symbol points or when the symbol loses its power to open up that reality for them.

The symbolic role of the minister may be broken in three ways. The Christ-bearer role may be broken, first, when the minister's lifestyle betrays the Christ who is re-presented. What minister is not woefully aware of frequent betrayals? After such failure the community rejects the minister's symbolic role because it cannot see the sacred through the misdeeds of the person. The symbol of the minister can be broken, second, when the community no longer believes in the reality toward which the role points. When the Christ, the call, and the sending of Christ-bearers no longer evoke images of hope and commitment, the symbol dies. And, last, the symbolic role of the minister may cease to mediate the presence when the community is blind. Willfulness and sin on the part of the people often blind them to Christ in the ordained one.

The Minister as Symbol

Who is the minister? A Christ-bearer; an image of God; a symbol of the sacred: all of these. Being a symbolic presence includes the whole of the minister's life, not just the preaching role or the spiritual aspect. In the role of symbol of the sacred, the minister must point beyond self to Christ, always guarding against becoming the object of devotion, making the symbol synonymous with that which it represents.

The minister as a symbol communicates on more than one level; this multidimensional signal makes it holistic and inclusive. The minister's presence addresses the whole person and communicates a message greater than can be put into words. For this reason, "being there" is more important than "saying something." Thus, when a baby is born or baptized or when a person marries or dies, the person of the minister speaks of the sacred presence without the necessity of uttering a word.

The peculiar role of the minister as a re-presentation of Christ had its beginning in the first Christian community. All the years since have influenced the meaning of that symbol, at times positively and at times negatively. Yet in the collective mind of the church there are certain expectations of the sacred in the ordained that cannot be avoided except to the minister's detriment.

The symbolic role we have described comes to the minister as a gift; it is not a standing for which one labors, or a claim to make for oneself. It is given through the call of God and confirmed by a community that receives the minister as a bearer of Christ.

Ground of the Symbolic Role

The minister as the image of God has a theological, psychic, and cultural grounding. By theological we mean that this symbolic role has its roots in scripture; the scriptures teach that ministers speak and act in behalf of Christ. The psychic grounding of this symbol occurs in the earliest experiences of the infant in relation to the authority figures who provide the sense of transcendence. The cultural sources of this role reach back to the dawn of consciousness when the human tribe recognized one of their number as the person who was in touch with the unseen world. A deeper look at these three sources of the symbolic role will indicate their powerful influence in the community of faith.

Theologically, the pastor has been created, re-created, and called by Christ to a special function in the body. We have previously indicated that these acts of God constitute the foundation for the pastor's spirituality; they also form the ground out of which this symbolic role arises. Of the disciples, Jesus said, "As the Father has sent me, even so I send you" (John 20:21). The Christ sends the minister as a sacramental presence even as Christ was sent by the Father as a sacramental presence. The minister has the task of equipping members of this body for their ministry of presence and action in the world. The minister is the agent of the head, the spokesperson for Christ, the model for Christian behavior and lifestyle (2 Cor. 5:20–21; Gal. 4:19; Eph. 4:11–14). The minister works as a mentor in the community, endeavoring to form Christ in the members.

The psychic dimension of the minister's role as an image of the sacred has its roots in the primal relationship of each infant with the caretaking person. In this primitive world of intuition and feeling, the infant's relation to the original caretaker provides the material with which this budding person later symbolizes God. The strength, size, knowledge, locomotion, and control of the parent image is godlike to the child. Beyond the reaches of personal awareness, this relationship provides the child with his or her primal construct of the God-person relationship.

This earliest relationship generates the images and unconscious expectations a person has of transcendence.[1] What does this psychic construction have to do with the minister as a symbol of God? The child's world is controlled by the authority and power of parental figures. In school, teachers acquire this role of authority and power. In the church, the minister speaks holy words and does holy things, like sermons and baptisms. By participating in this community, the child from the beginning associates the minister with God and sees the minister as the one who speaks for God. The distance from one who speaks and acts for God to this one being an image of God is short indeed.

The psychic development of a person with respect to authority provides the ground for the reception of the minister as an image of the sacred. As such, the minister plays a unique, though precarious, role in the lives of parishioners. This mediatorial role places the minister in the world of the parishioners' primal and most powerful images of reality. This deep, inner world of symbols is inhabited by both angels and demons. Thus to be a psychic symbol of the divine is a sacred privilege, a holy responsibility, and a role filled with danger.

What are we to say about those children who do not have the benefit of Christian parentage or early church relations? They experience the same encounters with parents as those who have a Christian context. Lacking exposure to the Christian community and to particular clergy, they may not make the transfer from the authority of parents to the minister as an agent of God. Yet the culture provides a deep, socially shared consciousness that identifies the minister with the sacred.

The minister as image of God also has roots in the culture. The cultural dimension of the minister as image of God arises from the depths of the collective unconscious. Resident in the social memory are images of holy men and women who mediated the sacred presence in those cultures of the past. From earliest times, every society has had its symbolic person to deal with the sacred mystery. The holy men and women mediated, appeased, spoke for, represented, and interpreted the Mystery. They were called by many names: medicine man, magician, witch doctor, shaman, and priest. All these consecrated persons dealt with the unseen world; they mediated the holy; they explained the unknown.

The role of the priest evolved as one who represented God to the people and the people to God. The priest had powers to appease the gods, maintain order, and provide security.

The prophet or prophetess also represented the holy. In this role the spokesperson for God resisted the dominant culture, proclaimed the judgment of God, and sought to change the social structure. The prophet stood for the free God who refused to be encapsulated in the dominant culture.

The collective unconscious, which is the social memory of a people, holds those archetypal images that have played their various roles in our cultural heritage. These unconscious images of mediator, holy person, spokesperson for God, healer of souls lie in the depths of the collective unconscious. These cultural images provide a foundation for the minister as a Christ-bearer.

Not only are these deep memories in the members of a congregation, they exist inside the man or woman called by God. The call of God activates the deep, unconscious expectations of the person called. Perhaps these deep memories provide the source of the unreal expectations that persons often have of themselves as ministers of God. Yet this collected wisdom of the human race is at work in the soul, creating the condition for the ministerial role as image of God. But these deep images can be perverted in an unscrupulous leader who poses as the bearer of God but is in fact a charlatan. We must ask, "How does this image and expectation affect pastoral spirituality? How does being a Christ-bearer, an image of God, influence the doing of ministry?"

Biblical Foundation for the Role

In order to become more specific in our designation of the role of minister as a Christ-bearer, we will employ the Johannine theology of incarnation and the Pauline model of ministry. These two first-century theologians have been brought together because the perspective set forth in John's Gospel provides an incarnational foundation, an emphasis that is implied but not stressed in the writings of Paul. Paul uses his own ministry as an illustration of the minister as a bearer of the presence of Christ, a model not contained in the Fourth Gospel.

Incarnational Theology

The Gospel of John offers an incarnational foundation for the symbolic role of the pastor. It presents incarnation as the way of redemption. The divine Logos through whom all things were created (1:3) entered into the created order (1:14) and revealed God, the Creator of the cosmos (1:18). The way of salvation in this perspective is through faith and knowledge of God mediated by Jesus Christ. He is the water of life, shepherd, bread, light, door, resurrection, way, truth, and life. These metaphors speak in different ways of Christ's communication of the holy to us. In order to know God, we are to drink the water, follow the shepherd, eat the bread, walk in the light, enter the door, share in the resurrection—salvation through participation.

Perhaps the substance of all these metaphors may be reduced to a single statement of Jesus: "I am the way, and the truth, and the life" (John 14:6). The way to God, the final truth, and the way of life come to full expression not in a set of rules or in select propositions but in a person. This person embodies all that may be known about God and about human life. Jesus is a paradigm of human fulfillment.

In Jesus' final discourse (John 14–16), he makes clear his intention to incarnate his life in his followers. Those who love him will obey his word; the Father and he will house themselves—make a home—in the believers. He says, "If a man loves me, he will keep my word, and my Father will love him, and we will come to him and make our home with him" (John 14:23).

In another metaphor Christ pictures himself as the vine and the disciples as the branches. They are to abide in him, for without him they can do nothing. At various times he describes them as chosen (John 15:16), as witnesses because they had journeyed with him (Acts 1:8), and as recipients of the Spirit who will tell them what to say because he will give them all the truth (John 14:26).

Christ declares that he has shared his glory with the disciples. What could be the glory of Christ except the bearer of the Holy in his flesh? He shares this privilege with his chosen followers, in whom he continues to incarnate his presence. In Luke's Gospel the close identification of Christ with his followers is made: "He who hears you hears me, and he who rejects you rejects me, and he who rejects me rejects him who sent me" (Luke 10:16).

These promises of Christ become the preface to Pentecost, at which time the disciples were made into the body of Christ through the power of the Holy Spirit. Participation in this corporate expression of Christ provides the context in which the minister is a symbolic presence.

An appeal to this incarnational foundation for the minister's symbolic role does not set the minister apart from the body of Christ. The references that have been interpreted to support our contention of the minister as a bearer of the sacred apply to all believers. Each believer is a home for Christ (John 14:23), a temple of God (1 Cor. 3:16), and a recipient of the Spirit (Rom. 8:9). In a corporate sense the whole body of Christ, the church, is a bearer of Christ. In the biblical, psychic, and cultural ways that have been noted, the minister has a special role as one who proclaims the word, administers the sacraments, and re-presents Christ. The apostle Paul offers one concrete model of the minister as a Christ-bearer.

Paul as a Model

The foundation for Paul's embodiment of Christ contrasts with that of the Fourth Gospel. He does not begin with the preexistent Christ who took human flesh and revealed the Eternal God to us. Rather, Paul begins with the crucifixion and resurrection events. The question he poses is: "How can sinful, alienated persons be reconciled with God?" The answer: "The old humanity, estranged from God, has been crucified and buried with Christ and new humanity has been created in Christ's resurrection." The whole of God's redemptive activity and purpose has been accomplished "in Christ"! This core idea of redemption forms for Paul the foundation of the church and of the ministerial role.

While Paul's vision of redemption stems from the crucifixion and resurrection, his image of the church is incarnational: the church is the body of Christ. The life Christ lived in the flesh has been reincarnated in his body (1 Cor. 12:13). Believers are baptized into this body. "Now you are the body of Christ and individually members of it" (12:27). The corporate life of this community expresses the life and work of Christ.

Paul's "in Christ" theology contains his vision of salvation. He contrasts being "in Christ" with being "in Adam" and shows the intimate relation between the believer and Christ. Paul says to "put on Christ" (Gal. 3:27) and speaks of the new creation in Christ (2 Cor. 5:17). He says, in effect, Christ is in you; you are the temple of God (1 Cor. 3:16). You have been raised and ascended in him (Col. 2:12). Christ is formed in you (Gal. 4:19). These references illustrate his vision of ministry. Through the death and resurrection of Christ, God has brought us into a relationship with godself.

Paul's relationship to the churches where he ministered shows the conviction of one called and possessed by Christ. He understood the role of the minister as a bearer of Christ's presence. And we must not forget that, for Paul, Christ is "the image of the invisible God" (Col. 1:15). For example, he describes himself as the "fragrance" of Christ and extends that to mean that the life of the pastor has the "aroma of Christ" (2 Cor. 2:14–17).

The believers are like a letter written on his heart by Christ in the Spirit. He can read on his soul the redemptive work of Christ, and that redemptive work is objectified in them. He states:

> You yourselves are our letter of recommendation, written on your
> hearts, to be known and read by all men; and you show that you are

a letter from Christ delivered by us, written not with ink but with the Spirit of the living God, not on tablets of stone but on tablets of human hearts.

2 Corinthians 3:2–3

He speaks of engagement. "I betrothed you to Christ" (2 Cor. 11:2). So the minister is like a matchmaker and one who prepares the bride for the wedding. The marriage symbolizes the relation between Christ and the church (Eph. 5:25).

Paul understood the new creatures in Christ to speak in his place. God actually speaks through human lips, giving Paul an awareness of Christ speaking in him and through him (2 Cor. 5:20). But the preaching is not of self, to lift up self, or to enhance the ego, but to proclaim Christ (2 Cor. 4:5), and himself as a servant. To the Thessalonians he says, "We were gentle among you, like a nurse" (1 Thess. 2:7). "Like a father with his children, we exhorted each one of you" (1 Thess. 2:11). Paul states that he was willing to give himself for these believers in Christ (1 Thess. 2:8).

Christ-bearers make no pretense at perfection; they have "this treasure in earthen vessels" (2 Cor. 4:7). When Paul affirms his role as the image of Christ, a symbol of God, he will not boast of this role. If he boasts, it will be of weakness, an experience that throws him back upon God. He has visions, but also a thorn in the flesh to keep his humanity ever before him (2 Cor. 12:7). The validation of his apostleship is his weakness (2 Cor. 13:3–4), because Christ was crucified in weakness.

Here is how Paul describes the minister who is the bearer of Christ:

We put no obstacle in any one's way, so that no fault may be found with our ministry, but as servants of God we commend ourselves in every way: through great endurance, in afflictions, hardships, calamities, beatings, imprisonments, tumults, labors, watching, hunger; by purity, knowledge, forbearance, kindness, the Holy Spirit, genuine love, truthful speech, and the power of God; with the weapons of righteousness for the right hand and for the left; in honor and dishonor, in ill repute and good repute. We are treated as imposters, and yet are true; as unknown, and yet well known; as dying, and behold we live; as punished, and yet not killed; as sorrowful, yet always rejoicing; as poor, yet making many rich; as having nothing, and yet possessing everything.

2 Corinthians 6:3–10

Paul knew himself to have a special role in this body as one who forms it by engaging persons to Christ, writing the gospel in their lives, speaking in the place of Christ, and letting his life give off an aroma of Christ in all the things he suffered for Christ's sake. Yet all was in dependence upon

Christ; even Paul's weakness validated his ministry because Christ was crucified in weakness.

To be a minister of Jesus Christ means to participate in his body, the incarnate presence of God in the world. This participation makes the minister a bearer of the revealing presence, a role shared with all the members. But within that body the minister has a role different from others—equipping them for ministry. The Pauline model of ministry makes the minister a temple of God, a speaker for God, a nurse or father to members of the body. This biblical image of the minister combined with the psychic and cultural material makes the role exceedingly powerful.

Stewardship of the Calling

Ministers who assume this symbolic role do so at risk. If they dare claim this call, this role of bearer of Christ, they risk confusing person and role. If they confuse person and role, they mistakenly believe themselves to be univocally identified with Christ and live an illusion. If they do not accept this role given by God and experienced by persons, they deny both the theological and the existential reality in which they live daily. This denial perverts, distorts, and confuses the ministry; by assuming themselves to have merely a secular function, ministers deny both their special call and its function.

In some eras clergy have tried to cast aside the mantle of man or woman called of God and to be secular in appearance and lifestyle. We must not deny our humanity, but at the same time we must not trivialize the ministry by making it another profession. Only by affirming the role can we recapture a portion of the mystery that seems to be lost. It is as detrimental to the work of ministry to lose the consciousness of symbolic presence as it is to lose touch with one's humanity.

But there are other pitfalls and illusions which the man or woman of God may encounter. The minister who tries to meet everyone's needs will become other-directed. If this vision of Christ-bearer is taken as a literal identification instead of a symbolic one, the vision leads both to legalism and exhaustion. Because there can be no higher call, this vision of bearer of the presence of God can also lead to pride. The testimony of Paul, who gloried in his weakness, offers an appropriate model. The human who embodies the archetypal image of God wields an enormous power, and this power can be easily misused for base purposes such as sex, money, and personal recognition. There is always the danger that the minister will live an illusion. One may affirm the role of the minister as symbol of the divine and still confuse this role with one's own natural being. This bearer-of-Christ role is not univocal. Ministers remain themselves with their weaknesses;

they bear Christ only through grace. Perhaps this grace of role is not continuous but momentarily at the discretion of a loving and free God. The burden of being the image of God sometimes seems unbearable, and every minister, at one time or another, would dearly love to lay that burden down.

While all these pitfalls lie in the pathway of the minister of God, it is our contention that he or she has no choice but to embrace the symbolic role, to live in confidence that the God who called makes each life a sacrament of the divine presence in the way that God chooses. This symbolic role pervades the whole practice of ministry. In the chapters that follow, we will examine this role as the minister structures time in liturgy and celebration, provides spiritual direction to individuals, and leads the congregation in its unique manifestations of the body of Christ in a particular community.

7 The Pastor as Artisan of Time

"You are the artisan of time, a sacramental presence!" The words ringing in his ears awakened Tom as if they had been spoken aloud.

Tom recalled quite vividly the dream that had awakened him. He got up immediately and wrote it in his journal before it slipped quietly into the unconscious.

In his dream a strange, eerie presence came to him. In biblical times this visitor would have been called an angel. He had strained to see her face and form, but the brilliance of the light caused her features to fade.

She spoke: "Come with me!"

At the speed of thought Tom traveled with her to the top of a gigantic mountain. At the peak he could see a vast purple expanse colored like the evening sky by a summer sun. Below he saw the city in hues of brown and gray as it was darkened by the night. This sight reminded him of the fusion of eternity and time; really there was no difference, but his perception had markers that separated heaven and earth.

His guide spoke again. "Do you see?" she said. "Time is but a measured segment of eternity. Time accommodates mortals with a 'before' and an 'after.' With God all is the eternal Now!"

Not sure what this profundity meant, Tom sat still, pondering quietly.

"Look," she said. "Do you see your church down there in the city?"

Sure enough, Tom could see Greystone Church.

"Do you realize what you are doing?" the messenger asked.

"Doing when?"

"Do you know that as the minister of God you are an artisan of time, providing order, giving stability, and creating a structure for the lives of those persons?" she said.

"I thought I was helping the people worship God," Tom rejoined.

"You are, you are, but don't you see, the structure of the worship offers the congregation bite-size portions of eternity? Without the week-by-week ordering of their lives, the days they live are circular, repetitious, without direction."

Then she cried, "Look!"

Tom turned his head. He saw a cloudlike Presence, the sacred mystery coming from eternity in the form of a man and joining with a specific time and culture. The union occurred through human consciousness in a particular person and a chosen community. The Holy One who joined himself to human flesh once, continued to join himself to persons in his community.

Turning to Tom, the heavenly messenger said, "You are the director of the drama that tells this story each week. This abbreviated history of God opens the divine mystery and invites persons to participate in it."

Tom recalled a seminary course on worship in which the professor had said, "Worship is like a drama in which God speaks and the people respond."

"Is worship like theater?" Tom asked.

"Whatever the metaphor," the guide explained, "through the liturgy you re-create the coming of God in Christ; and when you lead with sensitivity and openness to the Holy One, Christ is born anew in the consciousness of the community."

The idea that God actually used him to mediate an awareness of Christ, used him to speak to the people and transform their consciousness, their character, and their commitment, baffled Tom.

"Look again." The instructor motioned for Tom to focus on the church building again.

As Tom gazed in the direction of the church, he saw a giant screen filled with images. He saw himself on the screen; there were the Douglases, the Browns, the Thomases . . . his whole congregation began to appear.

He kept gazing and, to his amazement, saw a sequence of celebrations unfold, celebrations he had led in that very congregation: Christmas, Epiphany, Ash Wednesday, Good Friday, Easter, Pentecost, Trinity Sunday.

"These celebrations of Christ's life," said the heavenly presence, "structure the months of the year for the church family."

"What's this about?" Tom asked.

"It's about time! The structuring and ordering of time!"

"But why? Why the emphasis on the arrangement of time?"

"Don't you realize that without structure there can be no meaning? Without order persons fall into the abyss of nothingness. No terror compares with that of nothingness."

Tom shivered as he recalled the moments his own soul had felt naked in the face of eternity. "Forever, forever, forever!" it had shouted to him.

Still trying to grasp the ordering of time as a shield against the abyss of meaninglessness, Tom watched as his host instantaneously unfolded the life span of Vincent and Linda Thomas, a young couple whom he had recently married.

In a series of rapid sequences he saw their marriage, the birth of their first child, Vincent's success in the insurance business, the empty nest, illness, old age, and death. Their whole life cycle unfolded in an instant; the experience was like time-lapse photography.

Strange! He saw himself with Vincent and Linda in each of those sequences. At each turning point in their lives he represented the sacred for them.

The angel repeated, "You are the artisan of time, a sacramental presence!"

With that awesome statement, Tom awoke.

An artisan is one who practices an art, an artificer. A skilled craftsman, the artisan shapes materials like clay or canvas or steel into new forms. An artisan may be a novelist shaping a story, a photographer capturing just the right light, a jeweler who creates a ring that reminds persons of an important decision. The pastor is an artisan of time shaping the days, weeks, and years of persons' lives into a form that provides order, direction, and meaning. The work of forming the lives of persons in the Christian community is the creation of a corporate spirituality. So the artisan of time helps shape the corporate spirituality of the congregation.

At this point in our investigation of pastoral spirituality, the focus clearly shifts from the spirituality of the minister to the spirituality of ministry, from "being" to "doing." In the previous chapter we established the role of the minister as bearer of Christ. In the role of artisan, the minister structures persons' lives. These structures provide both the boundary and the substance of a corporate spirituality. In the matrix for forming our spirituality, we noted the role of time in the shaping of Tom's own relationship with God. In the doing of spirituality, we examine the role of the minister in ordering the time of the people's lives. The matrix shapes the minister, and the minister through Christ gives structure and substance to the matrix.

As an artisan of time, the minister serves as the director of the drama of worship, a structure of the week. The minister serves as a guide through the seasons of the Christian year, a structure of the year. And the minister functions as a celebrant at the passages of life, the structure of a life. In these three functions of director, guide, and celebrant the minister structures time for the community of faith. If both the minister and the people function self-consciously, these roles enhance both a corporate and a personal spirituality.

The artisanship of the pastor takes place in the present. It is always in the now time that we meet God, creating for us the "sacrament of the present moment." Time infused with a sense of the holy becomes sacramental time because it mediates God to us. This is true both for personal and corporate spirituality. How can the minister become the artisan of time?

This question of the practice of ministry challenged Tom MacGreggor to begin research on the meaning of worship in shaping the lives of persons. Ten years earlier he had studied the task of the minister as leader of worship, guide through the church year, and celebrant of the passages of life, but his present understanding felt inadequate. He made a personal resolve to reimage his role as director of the drama of worship. Tom started digging, making copious notes as he read.

Director of the Drama of Worship

Tom decided to extend his notes into a brief essay, "The Minister as the Artisan of Time." His host in the dream had said, "You are the director of the drama of worship." The idea excited Tom's imagination. Somehow the dream had made the truth of his role come alive; he had to formulate what this meant for how he led the people of God. The first section of the paper focused on "The Director of the Drama of Worship."

As the director of the divine drama of worship, the pastor orders the Lord's Day. The pastor serves as a drama coach, who prepares the actors, rehearses their lines, and leads them in the production. As actor, the minister does not assume a different personality. Christ has called and ordained this real person as the leader of the worship of God.

Worship is a real-life drama; it is the real life of real people being lived out in the presence of God. The drama consists of their whole lives. They are their parts, and the living drama is the actual production of their lives. They bring these lives before God each Lord's Day and, as a community, rehearse their parts in order to live their lives more faithfully. Their individual lives are joined with the corporate life of a believing community and are offered to God in worship, praise, confession, and commitment. And the community to which they belong also has its role in the larger drama of the human story.

The people come together on "the day," the first day of the week. The first day speaks of new life, a new beginning of power and purpose.

The liturgy of the Lord's Day rehearses the mission of Christ. The role of the minister is that of a symbolic re-presentation of Christ. Christ comes to the people; Christ calls the people into the presence of God; Christ hears the confession of sin; Christ offers words of assurance; Christ speaks God's message to the people; Christ invites persons to respond to God; Christ commissions the people of God for ministry and promises his presence forever.

The worship on the Lord's Day sanctifies the previous week and dedicates the one coming; it is a pivotal day. This marker day permits freedom through forgiveness and hope through anticipation.

Thomas MacGreggor had made several giant strides in being a minister of God. He recognized his growth, but something bothered him. As he thought about all these functions in time, he knew that life does not proceed in an even, unbroken fashion. The life cycle breaks down—sin, divorce, illness, drugs, the failure of children—and all of these cause the life story of the people of God to be broken and confused. He knew that he as a sacred symbol must enable persons to be forgiven and to forgive in order that their life might flow according to the purpose of God. In a courageous way he had to walk into the mystery of pain and confusion to bring order out of the chaos of persons' lives.

The minister not only directs the drama of the Lord's Day (worship) but also the central liturgical act, the celebration of Holy Communion. In many mainline Protestant congregations the Lord's Supper has degenerated into a memorial with about as much excitement as a book review. Perhaps we have overreacted to the exalted role of the Mass in the Catholic church. In doing so, we have lost a portion of our heritage and a sublime experience of encounter with God.

The minister as director of the drama of Holy Communion is also an artisan who shapes the lives of persons, persons who all too often bring to the celebration broken and marred experiences.

The Lord's Table provides the setting for healing the sick and reconciling the alienated. The minister, in the place of Christ, sets the table and guides the family banquet. In the Reformed tradition, the invitation is to come to the family table, to eat and drink bread and wine for the forgiveness of sins and for reconciliation with God and neighbor.

All who believe and have been baptized are invited. At the table, appropriate confession is made to God and to one another. The invitation, confession, scripture readings, and words of institution must be interspersed with appropriate silence for persons to reflect.

The words of institution—"This is my body . . . this is my blood"—mean more than a memory, more than a memorial. In Reformation faith these words do not mean a literal changing of bread into flesh and wine into blood, but these words do mean that Christ presents himself to us through these tangible elements.

Why do we eat and drink at this table? Because here we make actual in our lives the forgiveness of our sins; we receive assurance that we are members of the family. The past is forgiven and blotted out; a new day begins with the assured presence of our Lord.

The sensitivity, awareness, and intentionality of the pastor to this role of re-presenting Christ in the worship of the Lord's Day and the celebration of Holy Communion will always be a critical factor. Ministers must remember who they are and who they represent. This sensitivity requires the dedication to Christ of one's whole being, yielding oneself unreservedly to him. In a mystical, symbolic way the minister is a sacramental presence, communicating the real presence of Christ.

Never a mere spectator in this drama, the minister always fulfills a role as one of the people of God—speaking the word, yet listening; directing the congregation, yet following; issuing the call and also responding.

The role of the minister, critical as it may be, must not become inflated. The minister has been called to conduct the drama, but the people are the actors, the ones telling the story. They too are bearers of Christ, and the distinction between drama coach and actors is only one of function.

When Tom finished writing this essay, he paused to think what his artisanship of time meant. If indeed he re-presented Christ, what would he resolve for his practice of ministry? He wrote the following:

1. I will prepare myself for the role of worship leader through prayer and meditation.

2. I will offer myself to Christ before showing myself to the people.

3. I will trust Christ to manifest his presence in me and through me in the leadership of worship and celebration of the Lord's Supper.

4. I will expect Christ to interrupt the established order and do his work in ways I do not understand.

5. I will keep in my awareness that Christ may at any moment address me or the congregation through my lips.

6. I will remember that I am speaking for Christ, in Christ's place.

7. I will look at my hands as the hands of Christ when I lift them to bless the people.

8. I will remember that I am both worshiping and leading worship, that I am speaker and spoken to, celebrant and celebrating.

9. I will re-present Christ at the Supper in ways that communicate his acceptance, forgiveness, and empowerment for life.

10. I will trust in the goodness of God, knowing that my resolutions and preparations do not make the miracle of the divine presence happen.

A Guide Through the Christian Year

Satisfied with the first section of his project to revise his leadership of worship, Tom continued the essay. He was resolved both to reform his ideas and to make new commitments based on his growing awareness of God in his life. He continued his essay with a section on "A Guide Through the Christian Year."

Persons require a structure for the time of their lives. The church in its celebrations offers a structure for time—a structure that provides focus, movement, and meaning. To be without this "sacred canopy" leaves persons exposed to the terror of the abyss, a threatened meaninglessness that consciousness cannot endure. In the life of Christ the Christian church finds a paradigm for structuring the year. While pagan festivals were often adopted by the early church, even these have been transformed through an encounter with the gospel.

The Christian year offers the community of faith a structure for living a personal life in the framework of the Christian story. The Lord's Day is, of course, the basic unit of Christian time. It is the first day, not only chronologically but in priority. First, because it signifies a new beginning. The first day and the six that follow compose the basic unit of time for the Christian. Certain groupings of weeks stretch into seasons like Advent, Lent, Pentecost, and Kingdomtide. By placing these "seasons" of the life of Christ together, the church "Christianizes" time. The Christian seasons collect and order time in accordance with the events in Christ's life.

The life of Christ offers a paradigm for the Christian. As Christ is the incarnation of the living God, the Christian is an incarnation of the presence of Christ in the world. The expression of Christ in the world comes first out of the faith community and then from the participation of those members in society. As the community celebrates the life of Christ, it recalls the marker events in his life and restructures its life in accordance with them.

From the perspective of the church, the Christian year ends on Wednesday of Holy Week, and the new Christian year begins on Thursday—Maundy Thursday—with the celebration of foot-washing and Holy Communion. This is the beginning of the Easter cycle.

Easter is the story of new beginning. It celebrates the victory of God over evil. The fifty days following Easter bring that season to fulfillment at Pentecost, a triumphant celebration in which the church realizes the new reality in Jesus Christ and defies all forces that contradict it.

With *Ascension Day,* the focus shifts from celebration of life in the presence of the living Lord to the church's becoming his body here on earth. Realizing its impotence, the church therefore must wait for the promise of the Holy Spirit.

On *Pentecost,* the birth of the church is celebrated. The impotent, incompetent disciples are filled with Holy Presence and are sent forth as witnesses to the whole world. Pentecost symbolizes our empowerment for mission and ministry.

Trinity Sunday ends this season of the year by reminding us that God, who is manifest in three persons, lives in community. This season of the church year calls the church to be redemptive in human history. Christ empowers the church to be a sacrament in the world. "As Christ's presence in the world, the church manifests God's liberating, sacrificial, reconciling, redeeming, transforming love through the Spirit."[1]

This story of the church's action in the world continues through the weeks that follow Trinity Sunday. During these weeks, the church struggles with temptation, sin, and insensitivity as it seeks to bring its whole life under

God's reign. After six months of Easter glory, the story then grows dim and the church approaches the next season of the year.

Advent tells the story of regaining dreams that have been lost. It is preparing for Christ's second coming. During Advent, the minister leads the church in watchful expectation of the coming of Jesus Christ.

At *Christmas,* we tell the story of the coming of Christ, who he is, and what he can do in our lives.

Epiphany focuses on childlikeness. It is the story of a pilgrim people who live as dreamers and visionaries in the world. It is the period of the year for evangelism through the acts that we perform by word and by deed.

And this brings the church to *Lent,* a time to remember the human condition. During this time the church identifies with Jesus' temptations in the wilderness. Lent is a period for confession and clearing the soul before God. Yet Lent is always lived with the knowledge of God's understanding and grace.

Through all these seasons of the church year, the minister guides the members of the congregation in the structuring of their lives according to the paradigm of Christ's life. It is a fullness of life that includes celebration and rejoicing, confession and restitution, service and evangelism. Through the seasons of the Christian year, the community of Christ relives the Christ event. The people are the body of Christ; they are the continuing presence of Christ in the world; and they do what he has always done. The seasons of the year inform the corporate mind and bind persons together in a community of worship and service. Thus the corporate expression of Christ in the church continues to sanctify history by being present to and participating in it.

The faith world created by these celebrations provides the frame of reference within which Christians live their obedience. In the death and resurrection of Christ a new age has begun; death has been conquered and life has been given to all (Easter). The witness to this new age is the church, the body of Christ (born at Pentecost). In his absence in the flesh, it carries out Christ's mission to the world (Kingdomtide). Because it grows dull in this task, it must look for his second coming, his living presence, to enliven the community (Advent). Through the energy given by his coming, the church confidently evangelizes (Epiphany). Yet its failures drive the church to confess its sins and failures (Lent).

The minister as an artisan of time directs and shapes the lives of the people of God. For the most part the shaping of time is unconscious in the congregation, but it must not be unconscious in the minister. The shape of time must be made explicit both in the minister's life and in teaching. When these celebrations become conscious and intentional, they inspire lives that in turn give substance to history—lasting, meaningful, fulfilling the purpose of almighty God. The life of Christ provides the form of the corporate spirituality of the community.

As Tom MacGreggor reviewed these ideas about the role of the minister in the passage of time, it became clear to him that this incarnational view of the church's celebrations gave time a structure. The life of Christ through the centuries has offered the church a way of identifying its task in the world. Now, what will I do to make Christ's life present in our history? Tom asked himself. He wrote:

1. I will live the seasons of the life of Christ with the people.

2. I will be intentional in my living the seasons of Christ's life, and I will make the community aware of why we celebrate his life.

3. I will remind myself that, without structure, persons fall into the pit of meaninglessness.

4. I will use the major events in the life of Christ as a way of structuring the life of the church; in the present we will look back upon what is behind and anticipate what lies before us.

5. I will use the celebrations as a way to emphasize the aspect of Christ that we must demonstrate at a given time of the year.

6. I will enable the congregation to realize that through each celebration we incarnate the presence of Christ; we are Christ existing as community.

7. I will help the church to recognize both a corporate and a personal spirituality: we are the body of Christ together; we are individually bearers of Christ.

8. I will affirm to the community the hope we have that history will be transformed through the action of the Spirit in the witness of the church.

The Pastor as Celebrant

Before Tom MacGreggor continued his essay, he paused to reflect on his discoveries. As an artisan of time he was forming the spiritual life of the congregation by being a symbol of Christ. Weekly, he re-presented Christ when he served as liturgist; he spoke for Christ as a preacher of the word. As a guide through the "seasons" he provided this community a paradigm of life in the world. He not only structured time, he also "Christianized" it. To shape time for a community also meant to shape time for each member of the community. "Is it not genuine spirituality to live the life of Christ in our time?" he asked himself.

His project had become too rewarding to stop. So Tom continued creating a new image of himself by composing the third section of his essay, "The Pastor as Celebrant."

The minister serves the people as celebrant in the passages of life. There are seven major occasions when the minister has a special role in the unfolding life of a person. These seven moments or passages mark the particular times when the minister provides a sacramental presence.

The first passage of life to be celebrated is that of birth, the emergence of new life in the world. The celebration of birth places the pastor in the atmosphere of Genesis—a man and a woman share the creation of a new life, calling a person into being, naming and nurturing a new creation. As a symbol of the sacred, the clergy person's presence reminds them of the Creator; their creative power is derived from God. The sacrament of baptism at the beginning of life recognizes life's sacred character. Baptism declares that life comes from God, belongs to God, and finally returns to God. Whether or not the recipient understands the implications, baptism initiates this new life into the community of faith. The minister baptizes in behalf of the congregation for the sake of Christ. With baptism, Christian time begins for this new life.

The second passage is that of confirmation. Confirmation is the first invitation into spiritual awareness and responsibility. As the symbolic presence of the Holy, the pastor instructs the budding adult in the meaning of the faith that has been unconsciously absorbed from the community. Confirmation, usually around twelve years of age, is a specific invitation to conversion within the faith. It makes implicit faith explicit, and unconscious commitment conscious. In the laying on of hands, the pastor stands in the place of Christ, speaks the words of Christ, and initiates the young disciple into Christian awareness and responsibility.

The third stage of life is that of calling: that is, one's vocation. When the confirmed person graduates from high school and sets out to prepare for a life lived before God, the minister as symbolic presence commissions this graduate, in a baccalaureate service, to prepare for a life of humble service to God. The presence and words of the minister remind this person that one's life is to be lived for God to fulfill the purpose of God.

The contemporary church needs a formal liturgical celebration for those who are departing for college, trade school, or the military or to an immediate job. The focus should be on the gifts of the Spirit, the call of God, and the guidance of God in the search for one's vocation. God who created and called has a role for each to fill. This must be a festive celebration.

The minister as the image of God offers the supportive presence of the church, promising care to the fledgling follower of Christ; the offer stands through trial and error as she or he seeks a lifetime commitment. The theme of discipleship fits: commitment to Christ and commitment to one's calling. These acts demonstrate obedience to Jesus Christ. The exact liturgy for this celebration is yet to be conceived and developed.

The fourth major passage is that of marriage, a gift of God to perpetuate the race and to fulfill persons through the union of their lives. God wills that human loneliness be overcome through the union of two persons who need and love each other. The pastor as symbol of God's presence joins two persons, blesses their union, and provides an awareness that their unity has a depth reaching beyond the physical and social experience; their unity has roots in the very heart of God. Marriage, then, becomes another dimension of discipleship, acknowledged as sacred, transcendent, and blessed by God through the words of the pastor.

As newly marrieds reproduce, the cycle continues. Their first child is a symbol again of God's creative power; the creation of this new life demonstrates their co-creative power. The creation of children enriches the culture, enlarges the social experience, and makes business and commerce possible. Through preaching and personal guidance, the pastor helps couples understand the spiritual dimension of their role as co-creators with God.

At the end of a life of spiritual development, productivity, and social responsibility, persons approach the age of retirement. This event in personal history must be marked off for special celebration. One spiritual aspect of retirement may be the ceasing of one's work. The retiring person must deal with the loss of place and the lost of identity from work. Retirement years may be referred to as the "sabbath of life." Retirement may be a sabbathtide—rest from human work, even as God rested. In the later years old age may mean the relinquishment of the gifts which God has given. As symbol, the minister does not need to do much for the mature except be present as one who represents the God who loves.

This liturgical celebration, like that of vocation, remains to be developed in the life of the congregation. Attempts have been made, but the precise form has yet to be created. While these two occasions are less clearly defined and thus present problems, they are none the less essential for a fully liturgical celebration of life.

The final passage that demands the symbolic presence of the minister is death. Those who have matured must learn to say that it was good to have been and it is now all right to die. The denial of death keeps persons from facing the natural end of life. The pastor, as symbol of God, must always accompany persons into the dark shadows of grief, loss, and the no-more of being in the flesh.

In addition to these seven particular times of passage throughout the life cycle the minister fills another role unrelated to age: to re-present Christ as reconciler and redeemer. Sin and brokenness disrupt the life of every disciple. The minister of God re-presents Christ in words of forgiveness and assurance. Each of these redemptive moments constitutes passages in a personal life.

The minister re-presents the presence of God as no one else can. The difference between just showing up at the hospital when a new baby is born or a parishioner dies, and consciously being there as the symbolic presence of Christ, can be readily discerned. In each of the celebrant functions the spiritual awareness of the minister, the clarity about identity, and the intentionality of that minister affects how the role is fulfilled.

As Tom thought about the role of celebrant, he remembered his conversation with Jesse when his spiritual guide had said, "I think you'll find a continuing source of strength in an understanding of yourself as a bearer of Christ." Perhaps the older minister was thinking of these passages in persons' lives when he would be there for Christ. The role made sense to Tom, though he felt challenged beyond his competence.

In fact, the more he thought about it, the more helpless he felt. He could not make himself be a bearer of Christ. His inability stood at the center of his frustration. Yet he gained courage from the fact that he did not call himself to be a minister of God. He had been called by God. If God called him, God would be faithful to him. He could be what God had called him to be.

After this reflection, he made half a dozen resolutions:

1. I will be there in the crucial moments of persons' lives.

2. I will trust God to make me a mediator of the divine presence.

3. I will not question the validity and power of the presence of the minister of God.

4. I will not deny persons the experience of God through me even when I feel I am useless to God.

5. I will try to see the immediate meaning of a situation as well as the implications for the future.

6. I choose to believe there is a meaning to the call of God's minister that I may never fully understand!

In all these forms of sacred presence he, Thomas Louis MacGreggor, longed to be a dispenser of faith, hope, and love: through the direction of the drama of worship, to form faith; through the celebrations of the year, to inspire hope; and as the celebrant at the passages of life, to express love.

In all these times he would serve as the proclaimer of forgiveness when he heard the confession of sin and offered the bread and the wine as symbols of Christ's unconditional acceptance. As a bearer of Christ he would assure the broken of forgiveness and of a new start. Thus, as an artisan of time, he would express his spirituality as faith, hope, and love.

8 The Pastor as Spiritual Guide

About two years after the phone call from Jesse Van Meeter, Tom Mac-Greggor faced a new challenge from a desperate call he received for spiritual guidance. In the last two years his preaching had changed. He now spoke personally about the presence of Christ, the reality of a relation with him, and the interventions of his presence in daily life. Now he was destined for a surprise confrontation.

After a period of study at home, Tom arrived at the church office at 10 A.M. His secretary handed him a note indicating that she had made an appointment with a Cynthia Smith at 10:30.

"Who is Cynthia Smith?" Tom asked.

"I don't know. She seemed to know you," his secretary said.

At 10:30 sharp Cynthia Smith walked into Tom's office. "Do you really believe what you have been preaching?" she asked. Her question was direct but not accusing.

"Yes. Yes, I think I do," Tom responded. "What specifically did you have in mind?"

"About three months ago I happened into this church looking for help. You were speaking on prayer. In the sermon you spoke of God's knowing us, caring for us, and listening to our prayers."

"I remember," Tom said, "and I do believe that."

"Then please help me. I began praying that very day. I hadn't prayed seriously for ten years, but there was something in the sermon, in the atmosphere of the church, and in my feelings of loneliness and desperation . . ." Her voice trailed off.

"What happened?" Tom wanted her to continue her story.

"You can't believe how God worked in my life for the next sixty days. I hadn't spoken to God for years, but as I prayed I had a profound sense of God's presence. Things worked for me: my daughter began attending church; I met a male friend who seemed interested in me; the books on prayer I borrowed from the public library answered questions as soon as

I asked them; I even found parking places in answer to prayer." She continued talking about the profound reality of the Spirit in her life. Then she paused, an expression of disappointment clouding her face.

"Now, after the 'big rush,' it seems God has forgotten me."

"What do you mean?" Tom asked.

"My daughter who seemed so close to God a few months ago has left home; the man I thought was in love with me has made me a competitor with another woman; and the presence of God, which for two months was so real, has seemingly evaporated."

"What can I do to be of help?" Tom inquired.

"I don't know. If I knew what to do, I wouldn't be here." By this time Cynthia was weeping. "I promised myself I wouldn't do this," she added, referring to the tears.

"I'd really like to help," Tom said earnestly. "Tell me a little more about yourself."

"I was reared in a conservative home and church; I'd say 'fundamental.' My husband was a minister and served as a college chaplain. Things went well until we had a daughter. He became jealous of her and forced me to choose between him and her. I couldn't forsake my daughter, and the marriage broke up."

Tom nodded his sympathetic understanding.

"During the next ten years I earned a Ph.D. in computer science. I got a good job at the university where I still work. For those ten years I had no thought of God. I was for all intents an atheist."

"And?"

"Then at a very low spot in my life, I came to your church. I'm not sure why."

"And now you're experiencing confusion and questions about the encounter itself?"

"Yes, that's it. Was this seeming encounter with God real, or was it just a figment of my imagination? It seemed so right; I don't want to lose it."

A number of responses ran through Tom's mind: I want her to know that God is real; she needs to recognize her own immaturity; I wish to help her see that God did not die ten years ago but that an old structure became too small for her life experience. Guidance into these insights would take more than the fifteen minutes they had left in the interview. He decided to take a different tack.

"Let me respond directly," Tom began. "God is real, yet God has mysterious ways of working with all of us. Perhaps God wants you to grow in some new ways."

"Then you don't believe that my experience was an illusion or that God has forsaken me?"

"I believe God did touch your life, and I believe God is still with you in this struggle. I'm not too sure what this temporary feeling of desertion means, but I'm willing to walk into it with you and be with you until the light of God's presence becomes clear to you."

"Can you say anything that will help me cope with my feeling of forsakenness?"

"One of God's saints says that sometimes God seduces us with great joy and a sense of holy presence and then withdraws it to create an even deeper hunger within us. Perhaps God is preparing you for something more solid and stable in your life."

"I don't know about that," Cynthia responded. "But I do feel better since we talked. May I come again?"

"I can see you next Wednesday at ten thirty. Is that a good time for you?"

This encounter and the half dozen or so subsequent appointments with Cynthia Smith began Tom MacGreggor's work as a spiritual guide.

The Role of Spiritual Guide

The role of spiritual guide was not totally new to Tom MacGreggor. He had been guiding persons in their spiritual life since his first pastorate. But Cynthia's visit marked the beginning of a serious commitment to learning about this task and developing skills to help persons in their relationship with God.

As he reflected on his experiences of the past two years, Tom realized that what his old minister friend had been providing him was spiritual guidance. Jesse asked the appropriate questions; he listened a lot; he made suggestions when Tom felt bogged down. Without his support and guidance, Tom's journey would have been slower and more difficult.

How can Tom MacGreggor and other ministers become effective in guiding persons on their spiritual journey? What must they know? What skills must they develop? A historical perspective will provide the context for examining the role of the minister as a spiritual guide.

All religions from time immemorial have had their holy men and women. These early magicians, mystagogues, shamans, and witch doctors were believed to have powers in the unseen world. Through visions, trances, and flights of ecstasy into the spiritual world they predicted the future, claimed to accompany the spirits of the dead to their final resting place, and interpreted the mysterious occurrences in the life of the community. They used herbs and other concoctions along with myths and magic both to explain and to ease human suffering. In these earliest forms, the holy man or woman stood between the people and the Eternal Mystery.

In the Judaic tradition this role was fulfilled by priests and prophets, who sought to interpret the life of the people in relation to the God who created and called them. Through the law given to Moses they had a guide for life.

These mediators knew the Torah and spoke of God with confidence. They gave moral and spiritual guidance based on the law. In this role they represented God; they interpreted God's will for the people.

Jesus condensed the Jewish law into two inclusive requirements, love of God and love of neighbor. Essentially, Jesus shifted emphasis from a behavior motivated by rules to a life guided by the affections: that is, a passion for God and God's will. Jesus was perceived by the people of his day as a teacher of the law, an interpreter of the will of God to persons. He met a variety of individuals in their particular situations.

The rich young ruler came to him with a burning question: "What must I do to inherit eternal life?" Jesus did not hesitate to speak the truth to him. "Go, sell what you have, and give to the poor . . . and come, follow me!" (Mark 10:17, 21).

Nicodemus affirmed his faith in Jesus. "We know that you are a teacher come from God; for no one can do these signs that you do unless God is with [that person]." Seemingly without noting his affirmation, Jesus said, "You must be born anew" (John 3:2, 7).

Jesus' encounter with the woman at the well reveals a similar intention. The description is more extensive, the dialogue more complete, but the purpose is the same: to help this person find her relation with God.

In each circumstance Jesus helped persons achieve a positive awareness of God. All the actions of Jesus in teaching, preaching, and healing had as their aim relating persons to God. He is the primary guide and the enduring model for the role of the pastor as a spiritual guide.

After the death and resurrection of Christ, the Holy Spirit was poured forth upon the disciples, forming them into the body of Christ. Through the Spirit the risen Lord called and ordained certain persons in his body to provide spiritual guidance to the community and to individuals in it. There were many gifts and functions in this body, but at the center stood the task of enabling the community of faith and all the members of it to express the life of the risen Lord. Paul seemed to understand and appropriate this role more fully than the other apostles, and his letters provide specific guidance to persons in the churches he founded. Are we to think he was less a spiritual guide when he was face-to-face with his congregations?

The Pauline vision grew out of a vision of the crucified and risen Christ who took shape in the church; Christ was immediately present in his body through the Spirit. This vision created a specific concept of Christian lifestyle and a form of ministry that made Christ normative for a person's life and the life of the church. The ministry aimed at the manifestation of the life of Christ in individual persons and in the corporate life of the church. Perhaps a closer look at Paul's vision will be informative.

Paul's vision was grounded in the incarnation of God in the crucified and risen Christ; God was manifest in Christ and Christ remained in visible, tangible form in his body, the church. Every believer was baptized into Christ, put on Christ, and thus became a bearer of Christ (Rom. 6:3–4; 1 Cor. 12:13; Gal. 3:27).

This vision makes the role of the minister of Christ clear. The minister proclaims not self but Christ with an openness and sincerity that permits Christ to speak and act through him or her (2 Cor. 4:1–2, 5). When believers lose the awareness of Christ in themselves, the minister of God travails "until Christ be formed in you" (Gal. 4:19). The believer in whom Christ lives must put off the old life, which stems from the sinful, alienated self (Eph. 4:22), and must put on a new style of life, which springs from the new life in Christ (Eph. 4:24). A new being (2 Cor. 5:17) must wear the dress appropriate for the new life. This new being, received by faith, means more than a standing before God; it means a new life, a changed moral and spiritual existence (Eph. 4:25–32).

According to Paul this new life finds expression in the following behaviors: speaks the truth (Eph. 4:25), deals constructively with anger (v. 26), avoids temptation (v. 27), does not steal but works honestly (v. 28), speaks about the good, imparts grace and encouragement to others (v. 29), does not grieve the Holy Spirit (v. 30), gets rid of hidden anger and malice (v. 31), expresses kindness to others and offers forgiveness in relations (v. 32), seeks to imitate the model which God has given in Christ (Eph. 5:1), and walks in love as Christ did (v. 2).

Love, for Paul, sums up the whole moral and spiritual life of a Christian (1 Cor. 13). These character traits are expressions of love; they are also a description of Christ and thus of the followers of Christ. Paul expected every believer in Christ to mature in his or her expression of love. The facilitating of this maturity is the end result of ministry (Eph. 4:11–16). We are to mature into the fullness of Christ.

This incarnational vision of Paul reaches its zenith in his prayer for the Ephesian church:

> For this reason I bow my knees before the Father, from whom every family in heaven and on earth is named, that according to the riches of his glory he may grant you to be strengthened with might through his Spirit in the inner man, and that Christ may dwell in your hearts through faith; that you, being rooted and grounded in love, may have power to comprehend with all the saints what is the breadth and length and height and depth, and to know the love of Christ which surpasses knowledge, that you may be filled with all the fulness of God.
>
> Ephesians 3:14–19

Reflecting on this aim of the ministry suggests that the primary task of the pastor is to proclaim Christ, to guide those who are awakened by the Spirit into a relation with Christ, and to assist all believers in their growth in Christ. Disciples are to be contemporary expressions of Christ's love for God and for the neighbor. The clarity of the Pauline image leaves little room for question about the central task of the minister of God.

This vision has a mystical dimension: "in Christ," "Christ in us," "united to Christ," "baptized into Christ." These phrases refer to a suprarational dimension; they have a transcendent reference. With these phrases Paul gropes for a way to express the reality that we are united to Christ in a way that simultaneously permits us to be genuinely ourselves and authentic expressions of the presence of Christ.

Paul envisions more than mystical idealism. This model also deals with affections, an emotional dimension; with behavior, a moral dimension; and with community, a corporate dimension. The way persons feel about themselves actually changes through an encounter with Christ, and so do their feelings about God and other persons. This vision of the Christian life has moral dimensions also: Paul fully expected Christian believers to live a life of love; their behavior changed because of the love of God in them. This vision included both personal and corporate spirituality. Not only do individuals come to faith, they find their life in a community of faithful, worshiping persons; they are baptized into a body, a community. The task of spiritual guidance has both an individual and a corporate dimension. Perhaps this model has something to offer in the task of rethinking and re-forming pastoral care as spiritual guidance.

This model for ministry has a Christ-centered focus. These persons have been baptized into the community of Christ; Christ is the model for the living of their lives. The caregiving role of the minister intends to express the love of Christ to persons in their journey toward Christian maturity. Therapy, guidance in decision-making, and support may be roles the minister fulfills, but he or she should never lose sight of the goal of spiritual guidance in a person's relationship with God.

A Crisis in Pastoral Ministry

The previous two years had introduced Tom MacGreggor to a personal experience and to a role in ministry for which he had little preparation. The encounter with Cynthia Smith called him to listen deeply to her doubt, confusion, and searching. She wanted to talk about the reality of God in her life and the loss of it in her awareness. Five years earlier Tom might have offered her a bit of care or even referred her to a psychologist. At that time he felt so much discomfort with his own experience of God, he probably could not have listened patiently to her questions about prayer, faith, and the reality of a living Christ. If pressed, he would have had to admit that his seminary training had not equipped him for dealing with the Cynthia Smiths of the world. He had had a solid classical education in Bible, doctrine, history, preaching, and pastoral care. He had had virtually no direct supervision in his own spiritual formation or in the role of being a spiritual guide to others.

The experiences of the past two years created a crisis for Tom MacGreggor with respect to spiritual guidance and pastoral care. He faced a crisis of identity; who was he and what was his chief task in pastoral care? The crisis had three facets: theological, methodological, and stylistic. Each of these had a determining role in how he would now deal with the ministry of spiritual guidance.

Theological Aspect

The theological crisis was one of faith. What is the structure of the God-human relationship? The historical-critical approach to scripture, liberal theology of the early part of this century, neo-orthodoxy at its midpoint, and liberation theology at its close—all have lacked effectiveness in deepening the minister's personal experience of God. Each of these approaches enabled the proponent to restate, reappropriate, and contextualize the faith, but often the minister, or would-be minister, experienced the destruction of a naive faith without receiving guidance in the reconstruction of a profound conviction about God, self, call, and role. Do we not lack the clarity of theological grounding in the ministerial role exemplified in the apostle Paul?

This failure of conviction results in uncertainty, ambiguity, tentativeness, and confusion about one's person and role. In this frame of mind how can the minister be effective? And, still worse, the minister often multiplies activities to silence the cry of personal emptiness.

Faith requires the servants of God to risk their lives. Beyond historical criticism, demythologizing, literary interpretation of the Bible, a theology of hope, liberation theology, and dialectical theology there stands the irreducible Mystery of the living God. All these theological approaches remain powerless unless they derive from the minister's encounter with the Holy God. The encounter with God, reflection on that encounter, and the formulation of a personal faith generate the convictional power that provides a solid foundation for the spiritual guide.

The reader will recall that Jesse suggested to Tom MacGreggor that he examine the God-human relationship. Early in this second stage of his spiritual pilgrimage, Tom dealt with his own faith structure. Now he is confronted with the implications of his faith for a ministry of spiritual guidance for others. This ministerial function also fits into the matrix we earlier identified. In the matrix the self of the minister is formed; the task of ministry is the formation of other selves. The matrix shapes a minister's spirituality, and it provides the context in which the ministry shapes the spirituality of others.

Methodological Aspect

In addition to the question of God's relation to persons, Tom also faced a crisis of method: how does the minister offer guidance to persons on their spiritual journey? There are three primary options: psychotherapy, pastoral counseling, and the spiritual guide. Gerald May has made a comparison of these three models, as shown in Figure 5.[1] (I have simplified it somewhat for our purposes here.)

According to May, if I am depressed, the psychotherapist says, "How can I get you out of it?"; the pastoral counselor says, "How can I help you grow?"; the spiritual director says, "How can I enable you to find God's will in the depression and grow from it?"

Ministers must take care not to substitute uncritically the goals and techniques of secular therapy for spiritual guidance. As important as therapy may be, it can become a diversion. Ministers must not ignore prayer, discernment, affirmation, corporate support in the church, and the healing presence of the Spirit. We must not be embarrassed to speak of God as relevant to human suffering and need; when we do speak of God, our confession must have conviction. The urgent spiritual needs of persons in the close of the twentieth century demand that we recover our role as spiritual guide, a form of sacramental presence in the lives of persons who seek help.

The minister is not a psychiatrist and should not mimic this professional. The minister is a caregiver as described by Gerald May. When the minister

	Psychotherapy	*Pastoral Care*	*Spiritual Direction*
SUBJECT	Disordered patient to cure	Troubled client to help	A soul searching for meaning
GOAL	Resolution of conflict; adjustment to society (medical model)	Healing, sustaining, guiding (holistic)	Being and becoming in God
METHOD	Techniques of the trade to get desired results	Helping acts beneficial to the client	Self and the relation are vehicles of grace —letting go of blocks
ATTITUDE OF HELPER	Responsible for the cure of the patient	Client or relationship is responsible	God's grace responsible for cure
	"My will be done"	"Our will be done"	"Thy will be done"

FIGURE 5.
A comparison of helping roles.

deals with crises in the lives of parishioners, it should be against the background of the faith vision we discovered in Paul. The minister does not engage the situation objectively or dispassionately; ministers are never value free, nor should they be.

The spiritual needs of persons and the crisis of credibility in the church today both call for the minister to reclaim the role of spiritual guide. In reclaiming this ministry, we must keep a balance. Conservative evangelical ministers focus on personal spiritual guidance, often to the neglect of larger social issues. Mainline pastors too often relate only to broad social issues while neglecting the member's personal struggle with God. The urgent need for mature spiritual guidance demands that mainline clergy recover their role as spiritual guide without sacrificing their social passion. These two tasks are not antithetical, they are complementary; neither can live without the other.

Stylistic Aspect

How will the servant of God do ministry in the community of faith? The style of the minister can be informed by the Pauline model. This model calls for the proclamation of the gospel as a means of informing, inspiring, and directing the spirituality of the community of faith. The minister, therefore, must submit to this role in order to shape the corporate life of the church into the image of Christ.

The minister will also develop a relational style. This style means that the minister must relate to the people—know them, be aware of their needs, interpret the gospel so it enlightens their lives. This relational model inspires the laity of the church to share in building networks of relationships. Both the minister and the laity serve as spiritual guides who will inquire into the lives of the parishioners to discover their history, their concerns, and their experiences of God. How can ministers preach with passion and relevance if they do not know the faith life of the people? How can spiritual guidance be given from the pulpit when the preacher is ignorant of the stories of the congregation and of the preacher's own soul? How can laity share the ministry of spiritual guidance if they are not nurtured and equipped?

This Pauline vision calls for cells of caring in the congregation. A cell represents a small group of eight to twelve persons who agree to meet regularly to study, share their lives, pray, and participate in a ministry. This intensive fellowship deepens personal faith and enriches the life of the congregation. In these cells an understanding of the gospel can be achieved and appropriated in real-life situations. Questions can be asked honestly and openly discussed; persons can find support and strength. These cells of caring are miniature units of the church in which the Spirit works through each member of the body of Christ to enlarge the body and provide guidance for the individuals who participate.

To embrace the role of spiritual guide requires courage. This approach builds upon the existing model of pastoral care but reshapes it toward spiritual guidance. To respond to this challenge means to risk in answering God's call to a new form of obedience. Tom's new awareness of the meaning of ministry suggested the necessity of recovering this role.

If we explore these issues in Tom MacGreggor's ministry, we recognize the importance first of getting his faith straight; he is a man called by God to re-present Christ in the church and in the larger community. Because of his own personal crisis, he has come to a deeper confidence that God wills to be known and obeyed by all people. Tom's method of pastoral care, described by Gerald May, seemed inadequate in light of his recent experience. It was good as far as it went, but now he felt a keen desire to add the spiritual dimension. He was beginning to be comfortable with persons' spiritual experiences even when they were different from his own. He had begun to discover a different style of ministry—open, caring, vulnerable. But his growing edge at the moment was a concern to engage his membership in depth conversations and to introduce forms of church life that would nurture their relationship with God. None of these issues have been resolved for Tom, but he is slowly reshaping his style of ministry.

Agenda for the Spiritual Guide

As Tom MacGreggor reflected on his encounter with Cynthia Smith, he realized that the past two years had prepared him to meet her and to engage her life in a helpful, supportive way. His own awakening, his receiving guidance from Jesse, the new disciplines he had begun, and the serious ways he had encountered his own shadow prepared him for guiding others. Tom recognized, too, that to direct individuals in their spiritual journey was an extension of his role as bearer of the Presence, director of the drama, guide through time, and celebrant at the passages of life. These aspects of symbolic and corporate ministry provided the context in which he offered personal guidance to individuals.

In thinking back over his recent experiences, Tom sought honestly to find a way to fulfill the role of spiritual guide. What would be his agenda in offering spiritual guidance? In his journal he made the following list of priorities:

1. Recognize that Christ is the true director of souls.
2. Offer myself to be his agent with each person.
3. Listen deeply to the life that is being shared with me.
4. Look for signs of the presence of God in the story I hear.
5. Ask questions that will help the person seeking guidance to confront his or her life.

6. Share my own life with the person.
7. Suggest different ways issues may be confronted.
8. Respect the freedom and integrity of the person seeking guidance.
9. Pray with and for the person.
10. In all things seek the will of God.

If these were the preliminary tasks of spiritual direction, Tom also needed a picture of the journey of the personal life toward God. Without a broad view of the stages and transitions in the spiritual journey, he would find himself lost in a maze of stories and images. Two charts offered Tom a helpful perspective on the spiritual journey (Figures 6 and 7).

	Stages of Spiritual Awareness	*Worldview*	*Theological Foundation*
I.	Unawareness: Little or no thought of God	World ordered around self	Dead to God (Eph. 2:1)
II.	Conventional awareness: Church member; only attends worship	Culturally shaped world	Teaching of men (Mark 7:8)
III.	Interrupted awareness: Interest in God, question of death, meaning, values, asks ultimate questions of existence	Cracked world: Ordered world shattered by trauma	Reproof of the Spirit (John 16:8–11)
IV.	New center of awareness: Feeling of being drawn toward God; feeling of being repelled; fear of surrender, unable to turn away	God-inhabited world: Expectation that God will enter life experience	New birth (John 3:1–7) New being (2 Cor. 5:17)
V.	Split awareness: The positive interest is stronger than fear. Yet the fear remains.	Worlds in conflict: Old vs. the new	Wretched man (Rom. 7:13–20, 24–25)

FIGURE 6.
The spiritual journey.

1. Adolescence: The question of Christian identity

> The young Christian asks, "Who am I? Can I be sure of my relation
> with Christ? If I have a different experience, is it authentic?"
> • Often copies a mentor, imitates a trusted guide
> • A great deal of focus on self; a self-centered relation with Christ
> • Eager to convince others that "I am right in my faith"
> • Needs clear propositions of faith; relies on clichés and selected verses
>   of scripture

2. Young Adulthood: The question of intimacy with God, or Christian
discipleship

> The young adult asks, "How do I grow in my devotion to God? How
> do I get close to God?"
> • A desire to be close to God, mixed with a fear of being close
> • Fearful of what God might call me to be or do
> • Anxious about what to give my life to

3. Productive Discipleship: The issue of fruitful service

> • Identifies spiritual gifts
> • Finds a niche in the kingdom
> • Reproduces faith and life in others
> • Has little concern for reputation and recognition
> • Begins to be a mentor for others
> • Discovers the power of "letting go"

4. The Crises of Discipleship: The task of reevaluation

> There are two predictable crises in discipleship: the mid-life crisis and
> the crisis of retirement. In each, these issues arise:
> • Identity—Who am I now?
> • Loyalty and commitment—To what?
> • Production—What have I made of my life?
> • Time—How much time do I have? What will I do with it?
> • Priorities—What are my new goals and centers of value?

5. Mature Discipleship: The issue of Christian integrity

> • Acceptance of self
> • Being who I really am with others
> • A deepening unity with God
> • Patience with the failures of others
> • A clearer vision of the unity of all things in God

FIGURE 7.
Aspects of spiritual maturity.

These markers on the road to maturity gave Tom MacGreggor a notion of the various stages and transitions in spiritual development. Although he had much to learn about being a guide to persons on the spiritual journey, he responded eagerly to the challenge. He considered the task of spiritual direction central to the calling of a minister of God.

9 The Spiritual Dimensions of Pastoral Leadership

Tom MacGreggor was asked to lead a Bible study for the officers of the church. He distributed Bibles and asked each officer to read 1 Corinthians 12:12–27. Later he divided them into groups according to their assigned tasks in the church; they were to answer four questions drawn from this passage:

1. If the life and ministry of Jesus is the historical, normative event that defines the church, what is the church? What is it to do?
2. What does this passage teach about the role of members in the body of Christ?
3. How do you feel about being a member of Christ's body?
4. What are creative ways our church can express its role as the body of Christ?

Tom decided to sit in with the members of the worship committee as they struggled with these questions.

"How do you respond to the first question?" Tom asked Ruth McKnight.

"I'm not sure. Let me think about it," she answered.

Barry Stark spoke up. "It seems to me that if the life and ministry of Jesus define the church, the church must have some relation to him."

"I agree," said Robert Fields. "The church in some form is continuing what Jesus did on this earth."

"Doesn't this passage say that we are Christ's body?" Betty Brown asked. "Isn't that what the church is?"

"Can we say, then, that the church is the body of Christ on this earth, the re-presentation of his presence and purpose?" Tom asked.

There was a sense of unity in the view that was being developed. "Perhaps," Tom began, "a phrase from Dietrich Bonhoeffer will help us at this point. He said that the church is 'Christ existing as community.' I've been challenged by this idea of the church."

"I like that too," said Ruth. "In some sense we're the visible, tangible presence of Christ in the world. What a responsibility!"

"OK, if we're the body of Christ on this earth, what does that mean in practical terms? What are we to do?" Tom prodded the group.

Barry spoke up. "I suppose we are to do what he did—teach, preach, heal, comfort, forgive."

"Exactly." Betty joined in. "We are to keep doing in new ways and in different settings what Christ did when he was here in the flesh."

"If we take Paul's statement at face value," chimed in Ruth, "he is still here in the flesh, yours and mine." She spoke like a person who has received a startling revelation.

Tom suggested the group get on with the questions. "What does this passage teach us about being members of the body of Christ?"

"It says there is only one body, and all of us are members of that body," Ruth said.

"To me this means that the members are united to Christ and united to each other," Betty added. "Paul emphasized that to carry on the ministry of Christ we must be together in our efforts; division cannot be allowed."

"It speaks to me about dependence, or mutuality," Robert remarked. "We are dependent on Christ and on each other if we are to do what he did."

"I have the feeling that the members must all participate in the worship and work of Christ. There seems to be no place for persons to be on the sideline." Betty said these words with conviction.

"This statement of Paul emphasizes that all the members of the body of Christ have gifts; the gifts are distributed to clergy and laity alike. In this church we need to help each person give what he or she has to offer," Tom said. Noting that the time was getting away much quicker than he had realized, he asked the group, "How do you feel about being a member of the body of Christ on earth?"

"I feel pretty excited," Barry said. "It gives me the hope that in this committee he just might speak to me through one of you; he might even speak through me."

Ruth was quick to answer. "I feel overwhelmed. Me, a member of Christ?"

"I suppose"—Robert was choosing his words with care—"I feel a great responsibility to present Christ in a way that others will not be turned off by my example. The image of Christ in the world today depends to a large extent upon us."

Betty had been sitting quietly through this part of the conversation. "I feel so unworthy. If I am a bearer of Christ, I fail him so much. I feel really bad about that."

"I know what you mean," Tom replied. "I too feel that I let him down. Each day I remind myself that I am a follower of Christ." Tom reached into his pocket and pulled out a small aluminum cross. "Each morning when I put my change into my pocket I look at this cross and say, 'Christ lives in me.' Some mornings it doesn't feel true, but I trust him to express himself in me anyway."

The group had been dealing with deep convictions and strong feelings. The better part of an hour had elapsed. Tom was most eager for them to think of their work as the worship committee from the perspective of being the body of Christ.

"What does being the body of Christ mean for our planning the worship life of the congregation?" Tom asked.

"Applying biblical ideas has always been difficult for me," Ruth confessed.

Barry was one of the more theologically perceptive members of the committee. "If each time we meet we can think of ourselves as members of Christ, it will sharpen our conversation," he said. "If we think his ideas will be spoken by each of us, we will certainly listen more attentively to each other. As we recognize that we are shaping the worship life of Christ's community, I believe we will be more conscientious."

"I think as this congregation becomes conscious that they are Christ's body offering praise and thanksgiving to God, this awareness will make our worship services vital and exciting," Robert observed.

The discussion continued until the hour ended. Other work groups had had similar discussions. This exercise was Tom's first effort to teach the leaders of the church a spiritual perspective on administration and leadership, another aspect of his ministry's being influenced by a new sense of God's call.

Since coming to his first parish, Tom MacGreggor had had difficulty discerning God's presence in the administrative tasks of ministry. He loved preaching, visiting, and counseling, but he had struggled with his leadership role. Meeting with the officers, attending committee meetings, and leading planning retreats seemed more like creating a business agenda than being a minister of God. He had done his share of planning and administration in his real estate business; he had thought the ministry was spiritual and he could avoid the uninspiring tasks of administration he had resisted as a businessman. Now in this Bible study with his leaders Tom laid a foundation for interpreting leadership as response to the call of Christ.

Christ is the head of the church; we are members of this body and, as leaders, aim to make a visible expression of Christ in the world. Problems arise when we forget Christ, the true leader of the church, and our representative role. This absentmindedness causes us to substitute a secular style of goal achievement for the dynamic motivation derived from the call of Christ. An emphasis on the spiritual base of leadership does not denigrate goal setting and planning but, in a practical way, reclaims the centrality of Christ in the leadership of the church. We are not running a "for profit" business but leading a people called by God to lose their lives for Christ's sake.

Tom MacGreggor and other ministers of Christ who wish to provide leadership from a spiritual foundation must consider four aspects: their call as a gift from God, their vision, their pastoral tasks, and their leadership style.

The Gift of Christ

Tom MacGreggor did not choose the role of leadership for himself; he was chosen. The administrative function of the minister stems from the office of pastor, a gift of Christ to the church.

> And his gifts were that some should be apostles, some prophets, some evangelists, some pastors and teachers, to equip the saints for the work of ministry, for building up the body of Christ.
>
> Ephesians 4:11–12

Therefore, the role of leadership in which Tom MacGreggor found himself was not a self-chosen profession but a call of God.

The pastor does not administer the church for gratification or self-fulfillment but to fulfill the will of God. The pastor does not guide the church to gain popularity or prestige but to express Christ to the world, and depends not on natural wisdom but upon wisdom the Spirit gives. The administrative role of the minister provides vision, order, and direction to the life of Christ's body on earth. Administering the church as the corporate expression of Christ in the world expresses the spirituality of the minister as definitely as the role of artisan and spiritual guide.

The pastor re-presents Christ; as Christ is the head of the body, the pastor re presents Christ in visible, tangible form in the life of the church, no less in the boardroom than in the pulpit. Whatever the polity of the particular church, the minister is the practical head, the leader. In the congregational style of polity, the minister as symbol of God still exerts a disproportionate power in shaping the congregational mind. The preacher of the word speaks for God and thereby shapes the values, images, and direction of the congregation. In the presbyterian form of government, the minister moderates the session, reports to presbytery, and through a free pulpit guides the congregation. No other person equals the influence of the minister. In the episcopal form, the priest has the authority of the bishop to lead and be responsible for the congregation. In each of these polities the pastor fills an administrative role that cannot be delegated or ignored.

As influential as the leadership role of the pastor may be, it is a derived leadership; it draws its authority from Christ, the head of the church. Christ re-presents himself through the pastor in each of the three polities—congregational, a pure democracy; presbyterian, a representative democracy; and episcopal, hierarchical headship. While the polity may vary, the crucial role of the minister is undeniable.

Yet not even the call of Christ or the authority mediated through a church's polity can alone empower the minister. The spiritual power for leadership must always be granted by the people. The polity may determine the form through which power flows, but it is the spiritual integrity of the minister that persuades the people to follow. When the integrity of the person is questioned, the authority to lead is diminished if not forfeited. Therefore, the pastor must recognize that the pastoral office, though given by Christ and conferred by the denomination's polity, is finally confirmed by the congregation. By their response the congregation recognizes and affirms the pastor's gift of leadership.

In Tom MacGreggor's seminary training much emphasis had been placed upon the minister as an "equipper," the enabler of the saints for ministry. While the idea of an equipper, properly understood, has validity, in Tom's opinion it had led to passive leadership, the consensus of the status quo, and a loss of pastoral vision for the particular congregation. His experiences of the past few years had convinced him that the church required a deeper, more vigorous involvement of the pastor in the leadership of the congregation. But what kind?

The minister must have a *vision*. Vision suggests that the minister of God sees a positive picture of the future for the life of the congregation and its mission in the community. The congregation depends on the minister to be grasped by a vision so that he or she may teach and inspire others. While the vision may lack specific details, it is sufficiently clear to both pastor and people to provide a direction for the decisions that must be made. This vision is not a secret agenda that the minister hides from the congregation; rather, every sermon, every committee meeting, and even chance conversations afford opportunities to speak about this imaginative picture of the future. The effective minister always functions in the perspective of a vision.

Dynamic pastoral leadership also has the character of *passion*. Passion refers to the state of being acted upon by the vision; it is a compelling emotion that drives the minister in pursuit of the dream the Spirit of God has inspired. Passion moves the minister from the seat of a spectator to the role of aggressive leadership.

To be a person of vision and passion requires *courage*. Courage suggests a confident attitude toward the dangers and risks that the articulation of a vision brings. A visionary minister lives toward the future; this futurist perspective always calls for change in the present. The threat of change evokes fears and often resistance; thus, the necessity for courage.

The minister does not count upon these intangibles of vision, passion, and courage alone; the minister used of God must have a *plan of action.* Leadership requires forethought, definition of vision, optional strategies, and an assessment of the risk. So the man or woman called by God to lead the congregation must plan for effectiveness and follow through with the plan. What makes this approach different from businesslike goal setting is the awareness of Christ acting through the gospel, through persons' creative imaginations, and through confident pastoral leadership. As in the vignette of Tom's worship committee, the church seeks to actualize in concrete decisions the will of God. Leadership enables the church to respond corporately to the call of God.

Against this background Tom MacGreggor asked the question, "What have gift, call, and polity to do with spirituality?" Have we not seen that the cornerstone of his spirituality was laid in his call to follow Christ? If Christ places Tom in Greystone Church to re-present himself (Christ), is that not undeniably a spiritual calling? Nothing exemplifies incarnational spirituality more clearly than a minister and congregation discerning the mind of Christ in a particular place and giving expression to it through concrete initiatives. Discernment, planning, and specific initiatives undertaken with prayer describe the task of leadership from a spiritual perspective.

The Leader's Vision

The study of 1 Corinthians 12:12–27 that Tom led was inspired by an idea he had discovered in Dietrich Bonhoeffer's *Sanctorum Communio.* He had read the book during his seminary days but in recent weeks had picked it up to review the content. This early book of Bonhoeffer, a sociology of the church, spoke of it as "Christ existing as community." The idea grasped Tom with a fascination that did not go away. This church, these persons, are the community of Christ; they are the visible, tangible presence of Christ in this community, he thought. As he pondered the spiritual dimensions of leadership, this concept provided his foundation. The implications began to unfold in Tom's creative imagination.

The church is "Christ existing as community." Where is Jesus Christ? In the community that bears his name. These countless individuals have been called into a relation with God through him. They have been baptized into his body. (See Figure 8.)

The functions of the church are corporate expressions of the ministry of

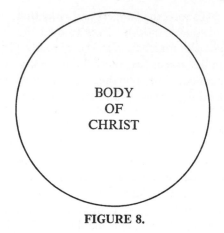

FIGURE 8.

Jesus Christ in the flesh. What the church does must be drawn directly from the actions of Jesus during his life on earth. Worship, for example, finds its origin in Jesus' going to the synagogue on the Sabbath, his offering of thanks to God, his fasting, prayer, and dedication.

The nurture function of the church finds rootage in Jesus' love for the children, his forming the disciples into a tight-knit supportive group, his offering of forgiveness, and his teaching the people and his followers.

The service function of the church is inspired by Jesus' ministry to the broken and needy. He healed the sick, fed the hungry, and welcomed the outcast.

The outreach function of the church expresses Jesus' concern for all

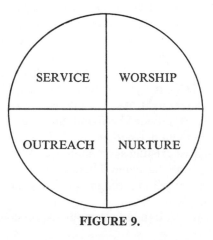

FIGURE 9.

persons to know and love God. His encounters with the woman at the well, the woman taken in adultery, and the rich young ruler and his calling of the disciples illustrate his coming "to seek and to save the lost" (Luke 19:10). (See Figure 9.)

Pastoral leadership aims toward a dynamic church—fulfilled, healthy, caring, a ministering community—that is, "Christ existing as community." The fulfillment of the body suggests that it claims and reclaims all those persons who belong to it. This filling out of the body of Christ is the evangelistic ministry of the church, a task that does not get done unless the church gives it priority in its plans. Without this function the body becomes deformed and eventually dies.

The health of the body of Christ demands the nurturing of persons' minds and the creation of significant relationships. Planning educational experiences, creating settings for building relationships, discerning and employing the gifts of the members of Christ's body all stem from the nurture function of the church.

Because Christ cares for persons, the church seeks to meet the needs of persons in its constituency. This caring spirit that reaches out to those in need expresses the care of Christ. The leader enables the body of Christ to discover ways of caring.

The church's worship is a corporate expression of Christ's devotion to God. When the church worships, it is a corporate expression of Christ bringing praise and thanksgiving to the Father.

Tom MacGreggor's reflection on these images evoked by Bonhoeffer's phrase challenged his old ideas of pastoral leadership. The church is more than one more group in society, more than a religious corporation, more than a social service agency; it is indeed the body of Jesus Christ, his visible, tangible expression on earth.

All these functions combine to constitute the body of Christ, and the corporate mission of this body is to "re-present Christ to the world"! This task of re-presenting Christ expands the mission of the church's role to express the values of the kingdom of God. The mission of the church at this point merges with the vision of the kingdom. In all its functions the church seeks to enflesh the mind and will of Christ, in its corporate life and in the life of the larger community. In this way it is a miniature expression of the kingdom.

The vision of the pastor has two centers of focus: the church and the world. It is the task of the minister to build up, or edify, the body of Christ for the work of ministry in the world. The visionary minister sees in the evil, injustice, prejudice, and greed of the world the aberration of the kingdom of God, the denial of Christ. In responding to these evils, a vision of the kingdom of God guides the minister of God. The pastor leads the church to actualize in history the will of God. In the darkness of sin, brokenness, and alienation, the light shines and the darkness cannot put it out. In a sense everything the minister does aims toward the manifestation of the kingdom; deliberate progress will not be made apart from priority, planning, and commitment.

Perhaps at the next meeting of the church officers, Tom will lead a Bible study on Luke 4:18–19:

> The Spirit of the Lord is upon me, because he has anointed me to preach good news to the poor. He has sent me to proclaim release to the captives and recovering of sight to the blind, to set at liberty those who are oppressed, to proclaim the acceptable year of the Lord.

A study of this passage might help the officers realize that the redemptive presence of Christ has at least four manifestations in the world: reconciliation, compassion, justice, and witness. These principles guide the minister both in discerning evil (the absence or the aberration of these virtues) and in expressing different forms of the kingdom (the embodiment of these virtues). As Tom MacGreggor thought about his leadership role in the church, he had an image of the church as the community of Christ penetrating every sphere of society with a witness of the kingdom. (See Figure 10.)

Reconciliation, compassion, justice, and witness are signs of the kingdom. In reconciliation, Christ reunites all alienated groups. The vision of compassion means the meeting of human needs: food, clothing, housing, job opportunities. Justice suggests the creation both at home and abroad of a new society that relieves oppression. Equality, a prerequisite of justice, is

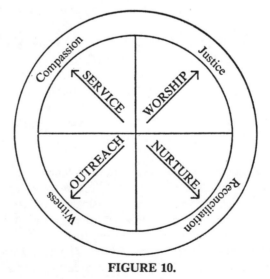

FIGURE 10.

the redistribution of power. It is the positive side of justice: creative and constructive justice. The kingdom is also witness: the communication of the faith in word and deed to each new generation and to those who are outside the church.

With eyes opened to the presence of Christ, Tom MacGreggor, pastor of a particular church, must be enabled to see in the concrete events of history manifestations of the kingdom. His task: to lead the community of faith to initiate, support, and expand the tangible expression of the will of God in history. This leadership aims at nothing less than the actualization of the kingdom of God in the present.

Participation in the will of God becomes tangible in acts of obedience. The task requires discernment of the presence of the Spirit and a risky response in concrete acts of doing God's will. The risks involved in leadership force us to acknowledge that all our choices and creations within history are ambiguous; they both affirm and deny the kingdom. Our realism recognizes that we cannot create the kingdom, even with the most discerning eye or the deepest devotion to Christ; we cannot perform the will of God with purity of heart or hand. Even our best efforts have their corrupt elements, and every manifestation of the kingdom falls short of the ultimate intention of God. Jesus reminded us: "It is your Father's good pleasure to *give* you the kingdom" (Luke 12:32, my emphasis). The kingdom comes by grace as a gift.

Perhaps it is an unfulfilled dream and nothing more than a dream, but the visionary pastor leads the church to shape its life like the body of Christ on this earth. This same minister directs the church in its mission to re-present Christ to the world. Such a vision transforms the task of "running a church" into participating in the incarnation of Christ in history. This dream was taking shape in the heart of Tom MacGreggor.

Pastoral Tasks

To actualize the church as the body of Christ and re-present Christ to the world, Tom needed to be a stronger leader. Already he was viewing the administration of the church through different eyes, but new vision alone does not create effective leadership. Previously, he had viewed administration as a necessary evil in order to perform the real ministry functions of preaching, counseling, visitation, and prayer. But seeing the church as a corporate expression of Christ had transformed the function of administration from the dull task of attending committee meetings to one of making manifest the presence of Christ. Effective leadership, he realized, makes the will of God concrete and specific in the world.

Tom now saw selecting, training, supporting, guiding, and evaluating the lay leadership as a spiritual ministry. The shift in perspective from the dutiful task of attending committee meetings to the challenging opportunity to build up members of the body of Christ changed this responsibility from task to ministry.

Tom MacGreggor had not been trained as an administrator, and he recognized his need for help. He did not wish to take secular forms of management as his model. He intended to keep central the mission of the church to lose its life for Christ's sake. Certainly John Swanson, a member and manager of an international corporation, could be useful, but Tom wanted to translate effective leadership principles into the new frame of reference that had been created by his deeper sense of call. John had the management skills necessary to direct a corporation toward its goals, so his viewpoint was important. He had also been vocal about Tom's leadership style. But Tom was beginning to operate within a perspective created by a vision of the incarnate Lord. The selection of leaders requires discerning the gifts and the call of Christ in other persons. The leader must help members in discerning their call, identifying their gifts, and becoming equipped for their tasks.

Equipping means enabling members of the body of Christ to identify their gifts and use them in nourishing other members or in serving persons outside the body. The minister assists the laity in thinking theologically about life and work, in developing skills, and in giving themselves in ministry.

The minister as leader has a supporting role. Members of the body of Christ need someone to listen to their stories of success and failure; they need responses of celebration and encouragement. Since the ordained minister cannot provide this support for everyone, members of the congregation must be prepared to assist. Committee chairpersons, for example, become part of the support system for Christ's ministers in the world.

The minister coordinates the work of the body of Christ. Good leadership keeps the various functions coordinated and on course toward the fulfillment of the church's calling. Without proper coordination, ministries conflict or lose their sense of direction. Structure and guidance give clarity and security to the persons involved.

Finally, the minister has the task of evaluation. The minister's spiritual role includes offering kingdom criteria that enable members of the body of Christ to assess their ministry. In a gentle, nonthreatening way the minister provides feedback and correction to members of the body of Christ. As Tom and John Swanson explored their understanding of leadership, they recognized a great deal of overlap in their tasks. But the controlling vision for Tom was Christ; for John, in most cases, it was the bottom line.

This vision of leadership will transform the minister's functioning, but it will also radically change the motivation of the members of committees. Recall the typical attitude toward committee meetings as just another job to do. "Nothing ever happens in committee; for God so loved the world he did not send a committee!" So often church committee meetings are dead. Too frequently we pressure persons to speak and almost force them to take responsibility. Glances at the watch and blank stares bespeak fatal boredom. Meetings are characterized by low energy among the participants.

These questions may spark a creative imagination. What if:

The minister saw every meeting of officers as a gathering of Christ's members?

The minister envisioned each committee meeting as an opportunity to hear the word of Christ through the corporate voice of the community?

The discernment of needs in the church fellowship and larger community was perceived as a call of Christ?

A minister believed that the decisions the body made would be a tangible, albeit ambiguous, expression of Christ's intention?

Would these expectations not transform the leadership of an official board or a committee meeting? If it transforms the task for the pastor, what would it do for the laity? For all the members of the committee?

This vision of leadership takes spirituality out of the private world of inner experience and translates it into a specific, manageable, functioning structure. The body of Christ acts corporately in the community, expressing the will of Christ in visible form. The church is the body of Christ; its corporate mission is to re-present Christ to the world. The re-presentation of Christ equals the mission of the church. In its actions the church expresses kingdom values. In them the spirituality of the church takes visible and ethical form. The minister expresses the church's spirituality—the image of God—by maintaining its life and leading it in making its evangelistic and corporate social witness to the world.

Styles of Leadership

Tom was challenged by the new vision of leadership that arose from his deeper awareness of Christ. Yet the question he faced of how to provide the leadership was crucial. What style would he use?

Tom began to think of the different styles of leadership suggested by the ministry of Jesus and the apostles. He could identify four forms: *coercive, competitive, consultative,* and *collaborative.* [1]

Coercive as a term has negative overtones; it suggests a directive, controlling, dogmatic, and authoritarian minister. True, the minister must at times exercise more authority. When, for example, the members do not know the nature of the task or do not have adequate skills, these circumstances drive the minister to take a more aggressive leadership role. But even as an aggressive leader, the minister must also structure strong leadership roles for the laity so that they exercise their gifts.

When taking a strong role, the minister follows Christ's example of clearing the temple, choosing the disciples, exercising discipline when his followers were doubtful and disobedient. Jesus was direct with the rich young man: "Go, sell what you have, and give to the poor . . . and come, follow me" (Mark 10:21).

Peter was coercive or confrontative in his Pentecost sermon. He said, "This Jesus, delivered up according to the definite plan and foreknowledge of God, you crucified and killed by the hands of lawless men" (Acts 2:23). Yet these same persons were taken into the fellowship and were fed and housed by the small core of believers (Acts 2:42). At times an aggressive role may be called for to strengthen the life of the body of Christ.

The second leadership style may be labeled *competitive*. In this style the minister requests information or opinions from a few selected individuals within a group: for example, a committee. By the leader's selection of these persons, the ones not chosen feel themselves excluded and in competition with the others for the leader's approval and for the opportunity to participate more fully. Competitive-style leaders must work hard to sell their ideas and strategies to their followers. While there is some inclusion for team members, this style still lacks openness and full participation.

The scriptures refer to Jesus' choosing three disciples for certain tasks and privileges. Peter, James, and John ascended the mountain, heard the Voice, and experienced the transfiguration. These same three disciples were chosen to watch with Jesus in the garden. Scripture does indicate that their selection by Jesus resulted in tension among the three as well as tension with the remaining disciples. Contemporary leaders who employ this style will experience much the same.

The *consultative* style expands the competitive style into a more positive approach as the minister continues to ask for information and gather opinions from more persons in the group about an issue or decision to be made. Rather than selling the group on a particular viewpoint, the consulting leader listens with an open mind and is influenced by the input provided by members of the body of Christ. Still, the leader does hold the final decision-making power. Consultation offers a sense of inclusion and power to the persons consulted, thereby enlarging the leadership participation.

Jesus consulted with the disciples. "Who do you say that I am?" he asked (Matt. 16:15). They provided him with information about what others were saying of his ministry. From the earliest days of its life the church held councils to discuss issues about which it had to decide (Acts 6 and 15). The minister who asks for information enhances the feeling of worth of those consulted. The minister also receives a larger perspective within which to make decisions. This consultation prepares the way for Christ to speak to the minister through members of the body of Christ. A consultative role exposes the minister to the word of Christ spoken through the lips of others.

The *collaborative* style opens the door yet wider for participation by the people of God in the decision-making process. In collaboration, the pastor functions with the group. Each speaks and each listens. But even in the collaborative role, the pastor holds the veto power. Yet this approach develops a high level of trust and participation in the group. Often the pastor is guided and persuaded by the information and feeling of the group. When the minister uses this style, the door is opened for all to share their gifts, to participate as equals, to influence decision making, and thereby to mature as members of the body of Christ.

Perhaps the best example of Jesus' collaborative style is found in the risen Lord's relationship to the fledgling church. On the day of his departure, he gave the task of witness to his followers: "You shall be my witnesses" (Acts 1:8). In this definitive act Jesus delegated to his followers total responsibility for the Christian mission. The ensuing pages of the Acts of the Apostles describe their collaboration with the risen Lord in continuing his ministry on this earth.

The collaborative style maximizes participation and places power in group consensus. The pastor does not lose power by sharing power, but instead receives greater power because of the trust and support of members. Certainly this style empowers members of the body of Christ and recognizes their full participation in ministry. Is this what Christ willed when he gave the Spirit to all, distributed gifts to all, and made us a kingdom of priests? The Corinthian vision of the body of Christ suggests a mutual participation in leadership (1 Cor. 12:12–27). This style commends itself to the Christian imagination, but it may be too idealistic for a world pervaded by sin.

In the practice of ministry, the visionary minister must select a leadership style that effectively meets the specific situation. A congregation lacking commitment, skills, and motivation will require a more aggressive style of leadership. As members of the body of Christ mature, they can and will share in leadership with greater confidence and effectiveness. Many mainline congregations today cry out for an aggressive leadership that is exercised with confidence and sensitivity.

The spirituality of the minister transforms the leadership role from drudgery and necessity to excitement and anticipation. The minister who has a vision of the congregation as Christ's body on earth, and history as the arena in which the kingdom is coming to fulfillment, has the foundation for effective leadership. With this twin vision the leadership task becomes one of planning and organizing the congregation in the power of the Spirit so that it more nearly approximates the body of Christ in its life and work. In order for this to occur, the pastor uses all the skills of planning, implementing, and supervising, but always with the consciousness that the leadership and organizational work aim at making the body of Christ effective in its mission.

The same principles operate in the church's ministry in the community. The focus of the minister's vision shifts from the church as the body of Christ to society as a bearer of the kingdom. The mission of the church is to proclaim the kingdom and to pray and work for its actualization in history. The spiritual depth necessary for this leadership makes it a ministry, not a task.

A great deal had changed in the ministry of Tom MacGreggor, especially his vision of pastoral leadership. While he was in the midst of the struggle to understand the spiritual dimensions of leadership, he went home one evening exhausted from the day's work. He picked up a Christian magazine and began reading a story that gave clearer focus to his emerging vision.

The story was of a young woman whose parents had been accidentally killed. The church they attended adopted her, cared for all her needs, and even sent her to college.

When she graduated, she returned to her community and requested the pastor's permission to speak to the church.

She stood before the congregation. "You all know my life story. Christ has done so much for me, I want very much to thank him." She paused. Then she looked at the congregation and exclaimed, "Thank you! Thank you! Oh, thank you so much!"

She went on, addressing different sections of the congregation.

"You are him, here!" she said. The grammar was incorrect but not the theology. "You are him, here!"

That's it! Tom said to himself. We are him, here, and I must lead this body to express his will and presence in the world!

10 Pastoral Spirituality as Servanthood

More than three years had passed since Jesse Van Meeter had called his friend Tom MacGreggor. Tom remembered well Jesse's asking, "Is it still fun?" The shock of the question had swept away Tom's amnesia and helped him remember his identity; it opened him to the continuous call of God.

Now the older minister had suggested that Tom consider Delos Franke for a series of Lenten lectures to his congregation. Jesse explained that Delos had been in a serious automobile accident about ten years out of seminary. Facing death caused him to rethink his life and his ministry. The result had been a dedication to Christ that transformed an egotist into a humble servant.

Jesse's recommendation inspired Tom to invite Delos Franke to visit Greystone Church. Delos's first lecture focused on the servanthood of Jesus. Tom was gripped by the text: "He came not to be ministered unto, but to minister, and to give his life as a ransom for many" (Mark 10:45, KJV).

As Delos spoke, Tom felt the power of his words. Like a knife cutting through fat, the text began to pare away chunks of pride and greed in Tom's life. The way Delos emphasized, "He came not to get; he came to give," convicted Tom of his vanity, greed, and self-centered life. When he tried to sleep that evening, he kept hearing the words, "He came not to be ministered unto, but to minister, and to give. . . ."

The next day as they talked in the study, Tom said, "I was deeply moved by what you had to say last night."

Delos responded, "I never think about the servanthood of Jesus without being challenged. No matter how far back you get in the line, Jesus always holds last place; when you think you have chosen the lowest place, he is beneath you."

Tom mused over the "last place" idea, trying to grasp what that meant for a minister. "Last place"—behind other ministers, last in denominational politics, beneath the persons in the congregation, last in line with the poor. Comparing the "last place" with "his place" left him with feelings of uneasiness.

While Tom took a telephone call, Delos excused himself and took a seat in the reception area. When Tom came out of his office, Delos was talking with a shabbily dressed man who was probably fifty but who looked eighty. Delos had one hand on the man's shoulder and was telling him about the love of Christ while his free hand reached into his pocket to offer money for breakfast.

Delos's visit demonstrated in instance after instance a loving man reaching out to suffering, hurting persons. The list included Nancy Head, a five-year-old who had been in a serious accident; the church secretary, whose son had been discovered with drugs; a hostess who in the midst of the meal blurted out that she was afraid because her husband had lost his job. Delos Franke was the bearer of a presence in each of those situations. Along with his words, his example spoke convincingly to Tom MacGreggor.

The prayer for illumination that Delos offered on Sunday morning summed up his spirit of service:

> O God,
> We commend our lives into your hands;
>   do with us what you will.
> Whatever you do, we thank you.
> Let only your will be done in us;
>   in all your creatures, O Lord.
> Speak through my lips,
>   that both I and this people
>   may hear your word.
> In the name of the Father and of the Son
>   and of the Holy Spirit.
>
> > Amen.

When the lectures were finished and Delos Franke had returned to his parish, Tom sat in his study and recalled the past few days. The phrase still echoed in his mind: "He came not to be ministered unto. . . ." The words spoke not only of Christ but of Delos Franke; Tom MacGreggor wanted them to characterize his life also.

In response to the challenge, Tom MacGreggor pulled down his concordance from the shelf and began thumbing through the pages: S . . . Ser . . . Servant.

He looked for those verses that spoke of being a servant of Christ:

". . . nor [is] a servant above his master" (Matt. 10:24)

"Whoever would be great among you must be your servant" (Matt. 20:26)

". . . taking the form of a servant" (Phil 2:7)

Tom's search for the role of servant had begun.

Christ, the Servant

Tom MacGreggor's investigation of the meaning of servanthood began with the person of Jesus Christ and continued with an exploration of Paul. He kept his reflections in his journal, primarily for his own enrichment, but perhaps he would also one day have the courage to preach on the meaning of servanthood. What does it mean to be a servant of Christ?

Christ is the enduring model for the servanthood of the minister. The form of Christ's servanthood includes self-emptying, identification with the needy, and self-giving. Christ emptied himself of the prerogatives of deity in order to join himself to human nature. The Philippian hymn expresses Christ's servanthood most clearly:

> Have this mind among yourselves, which you have in Christ Jesus, who, though he was in the form of God, did not count equality with God a thing to be grasped, but emptied himself, taking the form of a servant, being born in the likeness of men. And being found in human form he humbled himself and became obedient unto death, even death on a cross. Therefore God has highly exalted him and bestowed on him the name which is above every name, that at the name of Jesus every knee should bow, in heaven and on earth and under the earth, and every tongue confess that Jesus Christ is Lord, to the glory of God the Father.
>
> Philippians 2:5–11

The mind of Christ, the disposition of Christ, provides the model for the Christian. Jesus was in the form of God from all eternity. If anyone could have challenged God for equality, Christ could have, but he did not cling to his equality with God. Rather, he emptied himself; he poured out all he possessed that could have demanded equality with God. Instead of desiring a higher status, he gave up what he had.

He took the form of a servant. The Greek word for "form" suggests that he did not appear as a servant; he was a servant in essence; literally, a slave. Christ chose the servant role to reveal the hidden nature of God. How shocking! Deity serves.

Christ was born in the likeness of human beings. Paul described how

Christ looked to humans. He did not mean that Christ only appeared to be human, as some in his day insisted; he *was* human.

And as a human being, Christ humbled himself. He claimed no power or position for himself; he counted others higher and better; he recognized limitations. But humility is not self-flagellation.

As an obedient servant, Christ recognized an authority greater than his own; he submitted himself to the authority of Another who had the right to direct him. Christ did not grasp his equality with God but emptied himself of privilege; his obedience to God demonstrates the continual recognition of the power of Another over him.

The phrase "unto death, even death on a cross," suggests the extent of Christ's obedience. A weak obedience fades in the face of persecution or pain, but Christ's obedience did not waver even in the face of death. Steadfastly, he obeyed to the end.

Between the self-emptying of Christ and his death on a cross lies his ministry. Bounded by renunciation at the beginning and self-sacrifice at the end, his acts of compassion and mercy were punctuated with the spirit of servanthood. Identification with humanity and service to human need characterized his revelation of God to people.

Christ emptied himself of the prerogatives of deity so that as a human being he might identify with those whom he came to serve—the sinful, the poor, the powerless, the marginalized, and the religious, the powerful, the leaders. The symbol of his complete identification with them is baptism.

> Then Jesus came from Galilee to the Jordan to John, to be baptized by him. John would have prevented him, saying, "I need to be baptized by you, and do you come to me?"
>
> But Jesus answered him, "Let it be so now; for thus it is fitting for us to fulfil all righteousness."
>
> Then he consented. And when Jesus was baptized, he went up immediately from the water, and behold, the heavens were opened and he saw the Spirit of God descending like a dove, and alighting on him; and lo, a voice from heaven, saying, "This is my beloved Son, with whom I am well pleased."
>
> Matthew 3:13–17

Jesus insisted on baptism from John because it was his way of announcing his identification with suffering humanity. In this moment of baptism Jesus became one with all the broken, sinful, and marginalized. By being baptized, Jesus placed himself beside all types of persons. The way of reconciliation and redemption is by identification.

In his ministry Jesus demonstrated the role of a servant. Evidence from the gospels suggests that he served all those with whom he had become identified at John's baptism. The enduring sign of his servanthood occurred in the upper room just before his death (John 13:3–11).

Jesus rose from the table, took the towel and basin, and knelt before each of his followers to wash their feet. He washed the feet of his betrayer, of another who denied him, of ten who forsook him in the time of testing.

He furthermore exhorted his disciples, saying, "I have given you an example, that you also should do as I have done to you" (John 13:15). Jesus urged his disciples to follow the pattern he had laid out. "A servant is not greater than his master. . . . A new commandment I give to you, that you love one another; even as I have loved you, that you also love one another" (John 3:16, 34). This loving servanthood is the identifying mark of discipleship. "By this all men will know that you are my disciples, if you have love for one another" (John 13:35).

Jesus is the model for the minister-servant. If we take his model as a directive from God, whatever privilege the minister may have must be renounced; identification with humanity must be chosen and the pathway of obedience followed even to death. But we must be clear about a central point; he was the servant of God! His self-renunciation, self-emptying, and self-effacement were directed toward God. He served God through serving persons. The sequence was: servant of God, servant of the people. To reverse the sequence would have had the disastrous consequence of making him subject to every human wish or demand.

The hinge word in the Philippians passage is "therefore": "Therefore God has highly exalted him" (Phil. 2:9). On one side of this word swings the downward movement of Christ to sinful humanity; on the other, the elevation of Christ to the right hand of God through the power of resurrection. "Therefore God has . . ." God does not act because of the relinquishment of Christ or because of his self-emptying, identification, and obedience. God acts out of sovereign freedom. God can do no other and be God, for this is God's own nature.

So God exalts the Son, gives him a name above every name, and calls heaven and earth to confess that "Jesus Christ is Lord." The self-sacrifice of the servant of God never goes unnoticed by God. God exalts the servant at the proper time.

The Pauline Model

This model of self-emptying servanthood inspired and shaped the apostolic ministry of Paul. Perhaps it was the Philippian hymn that inspired his own self-emptying. After describing the self-emptying of Christ, he wrote of his own self-renunciation:

For we are the true circumcision, who worship God in spirit, and glory in Christ Jesus, and put no confidence in the flesh. Though I myself have reason for confidence in the flesh also. If any other man thinks he has reason for confidence in the flesh, I have more: circumcised on the eighth day, of the people of Israel, of the tribe of Benjamin, a Hebrew born of Hebrews; as to the law a Pharisee, as to zeal a persecutor of the church, as to righteousness under the law blameless. But whatever gain I had, I counted as loss for the sake of Christ. Indeed I count everything as loss because of the surpassing worth of knowing Christ Jesus my Lord. For his sake I have suffered the loss of all things, and count them as refuse, in order that I may gain Christ and be found in him, not having a righteousness of my own, based on law, but that which is through faith in Christ, the righteousness from God that depends on faith; that I may know him and the power of his resurrection, and may share his sufferings, becoming like him in his death, that if possible I may attain the resurrection from the dead.

                                                              Philippians 3:3–11

This confession of the apostle takes on greater significance against the background of the hymn in Philippians 2. Paul compared his relation to Israel with Christ's relation to God. He had all the natural gifts and performances that would make him acceptable to God. But he placed no confidence in natural or cultural or material gifts to gain God's approval. His credits included: circumcised the eighth day, of the Hebrew people, of the tribe of Benjamin, a Hebrew among Hebrews, blameless before the law, a persecutor of the church. Yet he counted everything as dung, waste, refuse, in order that he might gain the knowledge of Jesus Christ.

Paul placed himself in dependence upon God. "Therefore God has ..." A pivotal moment in Christ's ministry was also crucial for the apostle. He awaited the direct action of God to use his self-emptying in whatever way God chose.

Like Christ, Paul identified with those whom he served. When Paul preached to the Thessalonians, he worked as they did, lived a life of holiness, loved and exhorted them like a father.

For you remember our labor and toil, brethren; we worked night and day, that we might not burden any of you, while we preached to you the gospel of God. You are witnesses, and God also, how holy and righteous and blameless was our behavior to you believers; for you know how, like a father with his children, we exhorted each one of you and encouraged you and charged you to lead a life worthy of God, who calls you into his own kingdom and glory.

                                                        1 Thessalonians 2:9–12

Paul identified with all to whom he preached. He identified with Jews in order to win the Jews; to those who were under the law, he became as under the law. And to those outside the law, as one without the law. With the weak he became as weak (1 Cor. 9:19–23): "I have made myself a slave to all, that I might win the more" (v. 19).

Paul chose the role of servant. He was always the servant of Christ in serving the people. Note the sequence again: servant of Christ, servant of the people. Paul had only one authority—Christ; he had only one person to please—Christ; one agenda—to serve Christ by serving people. Herein lies the difference between ministry and social service. Paul envisioned the meeting of human need as visible service to Jesus Christ. He upheld and affirmed servanthood to Christ as the model for ministry. He said, "This is how one should regard us, as servants of Christ and stewards of the mysteries of God" (1 Cor. 4:1). He asserted, "For though I am free from all men, I have made myself a slave to all" (1 Cor. 9:19). He further testified, "For what we preach is not ourselves, but Jesus Christ as Lord, with ourselves as your servants for Jesus' sake" (2 Cor. 4:5).

With dogged determination Paul followed the Christ who emptied himself and took the form of a servant.

Yet Paul protected his servanthood from misunderstanding. He wanted no obstacle to faith or life to arise from his lifestyle; he wished always to commend himself and the ministry of Christ to others:

> We put no obstacle in any one's way, so that no fault may be found with our ministry, but as servants of God we commend ourselves in every way: through great endurance, in afflictions, hardships, calamities, beatings, imprisonments, tumults, labors, watching, hunger; by purity, knowledge, forbearance, kindness, the Holy Spirit, genuine love, truthful speech, and the power of God; with the weapons of righteousness for the right hand and for the left; in honor and dishonor, in ill repute and good repute. We are treated as imposters, and yet are true; as unknown, and yet well known; as dying, and behold we live; as punished, and yet not killed; as sorrowful, yet always rejoicing; as poor, yet making many rich; as having nothing, and yet possessing everything.
>
> 2 Corinthians 6:3–10

For My Ministry

As Tom MacGreggor thought about the primary model of Jesus as servant and the example of Paul as a servant, he made the following resolutions.

1. As the servant of Jesus Christ, I have nothing to commend me to God or to people. I cannot depend on my family heritage, my educational preparation, my natural gifts, my acquired skill and experience, or my role as a minister. Jesus' model suggests that I must empty myself of all that

naturally commends me so that I might hope for God's commendation. Like Paul, I count these things as refuse that I may gain Christ. If I depend on my own powers, I cannot count on the power of Christ.

2. As the servant of Christ I will identify with those to whom I minister. I will relate to the minorities who are beginning to move into our community. I will learn their names, sit in their homes, talk with them about their concerns. I will care also about the new leadership in the city. I will be identified with the marginalized, the poor, the powerless in my community. But I will also minister to the middle class, the educated, the wealthy.

In the matrix through which Christ has served me, I now serve him. I am his servant, mediating his presence to persons in worship; I am serving Christ through the ministries we have to the community; I serve him in the present moment; and, in a way beyond my comprehension, I am a small part of the fulfillment of his will in human history.

3. Christ, the servant of God; Paul, the servant of Christ; Tom MacGreggor, a servant also. I am the servant of all. I will take the towel and basin and wash their feet. I will offer myself to them in the meeting of their needs. And when I serve the needs of others, I will look for the image of Christ in them, for in serving them I am serving him (Matt. 25:40). I follow him who said, "I am among you as one who serves" (Luke 22:27). But I will keep the priority in order: servant of Christ, servant of the people.

Servanthood: Crucifixion and Resurrection

As we investigate the role of servant, we discover that servanthood operates in the tension between crucifixion and resurrection. This paradox in the servanthood of Jesus was represented by the emptying of self on the one side and the exaltation of his name on the other. In the ministry of Paul the paradox is represented in counting as dung his natural achievements and his great desire to possess the knowledge of Christ.

In this tension, crucifixion means vulnerability, exposure to suffering, the threat of death; resurrection means courage in the presence of opposition, helplessness met with divine power, the threat of death met with triumph over the powers of evil.

As Tom reflected on this tension, he sought to apply to his ministry the insight he had gained. He wrote in his journal:

As the bearer of Christ I am exposed to the anger, frustration, and disappointment of persons. They unconsciously project on me their disappointment with God. Do I not share in the crucifixion in some small way when I absorb the anger and frustration of the disillusioned? Cannot I hope for the power of resurrection that enables me to forgive those "who know not what they do"?

As the artisan of time I am identified with the congregation's losses (death, illness, empty nest, retirement, failing health) and their triumphs (birth, life, marriage, success, honor). I am there giving visible, tangible expression of the Lord's presence at the significant times in their lives. In the first instance I share Christ's crucifixion as I feel their sufferings. In the latter I share his joy in being exalted by the Lord God. Perhaps this is what Paul meant when he spoke of sharing in the resurrection.

As a spiritual guide I have the opportunity to walk into the darkness and pain of persons' lives. The crucifixion represents darkness when Christ walked into the blackness of alienation from the Father; it is crucifixion when we engage the darkness. Yet I am confident that the Lord is present in the darkness and transforms it by the light of the resurrection. I dare to speak of light in the darkness only because of a confidence in the resurrection.

As a leader of the community of faith, I may suffer rejection and rebuff from the powerful. I may be exposed to death for a witness to justice; the world has always crucified the faithful witness who refuses to legitimate the status quo. Yet the resurrection appears as the breaking in of the kingdom for the oppressed and suffering, the weak and the marginalized.

I believe Paul aptly summed up the meaning of the ministry that exists in this incredible tension:

"For what we preach is not ourselves, but Jesus Christ as Lord, with ourselves as your servants for Jesus' sake. For it is the God who said, 'Let light shine out of darkness,' who has shone in our hearts to give the light of the knowledge of the glory of God in the face of Christ.

"But we have this treasure in earthen vessels, to show that the transcendent power belongs to God and not to us. We are afflicted in every way, but not crushed; perplexed, but not driven to despair; persecuted, but not forsaken; struck down, but not destroyed; always carrying in the body the death of Jesus, so that the life of Jesus may also be manifested in our bodies. For while we live we are always being given up to death for Jesus' sake, so that the life of Jesus may be manifested in our mortal flesh. So death is at work in us, but life in you" (2 Cor. 4:5–12).

Crucifixion reveals the essential meaning of servanthood. Crucifixion means the loss of power—institutional, political, social, financial, and intellectual power. The person exposed to death on the cross has sacrificed all power. This affirmation does not depreciate the creature bearing God's image. The minister cannot do this ministry of God apart from divine grace and the initiative of the Holy Spirit.

To become obedient to another, to serve another, means the voluntary sacrifice of one's own powers. In obedience, the servant of Christ lays aside what could legitimately be held and claimed for oneself. This act of obedience, which gives up self, at the same time offers fulfillment.

No one voluntarily chooses crucifixion; no one intentionally seeks pain. But when the call and compulsion of one's convictions demand it, the choice to suffer must be made. When that moment arrives, the faithful minister must not run away from the cross.

Crucifixion is the ultimate act of servanthood. In crucifixion we are emptied, identified with the broken and alienated, and offered the service that ultimately reshapes the world. Beyond this act of complete self-abnegation there is a power—resurrection. Self-sacrifice means the total loss of power, but in the act of giving up power, a new power emerges. This power exceeds in kind the power that the minister relinquishes because resurrection is a greater power.

Christ's relinquishment of power did not merit the gift of power. The power was given him. In response to Christ's self-emptying, God acted in freedom and grace. The crucified does not control the power. Neither Jesus nor Gandhi nor King manipulated the power that was released through their self-giving. But the cross does release a moral power that attacks injustice at its core. This moral power possesses a life and direction of its own, maybe a manifestation of the Moral itself. The sacrifice of self is irresistible in its moral appeal. Sacrifice, when recognized by others, provides a controlling influence in their lives.

These insights illuminated Tom's life like bolts of lightning. He felt an almost overwhelming sense of excitement about his new perspective on ministry, but he also acknowledged to himself that he was afraid. Could he really become the servant of Christ he wanted to be? Could he face his own crucifixion? He turned to God in prayer:

> O God,
> In the midst of this reflection it seems so clear
>   what I am to be for the sake of Christ:
> A servant who gives his life for his Lord
>   and for the people he has been called to serve.
> Give me strength to live in this tension.
> Give me courage when I am afraid.
> Support me with faith when doubts overwhelm me.
> Keep me steadfast when I would seek an easier way.
> Amen.

Crucifixion and Self-Realization

What does this total surrender mean for Tom? Does it mean a loss of self, or genuine self-fulfillment? Does crucifixion contradict self-realization and self-fulfillment? The spirit of the age has been the quest for self-fulfillment through lust, greed, and self-expression without restraint. In many instances self-fulfillment has become a religion; in fact, the cult of self-actualization has included many of the clergy. So often the promise of humanistic self-realization exceeds its ability to fulfill. From a biblical perspective this quest for self and its actualization can be realized only in self-surrender and self-dedication.

Jesus stands as a constant reminder to us that "he who finds his life will lose it." Yet the loss of self cannot be a reality until there is a self to be lost. Thus one must form a firm identity that can be freely offered to God. Only the fully formed person who has both a self and a will may pray with integrity, "Not my will, but thine, be done." To pray this prayer without a will of one's own covers over weakness and immaturity.

Our contention has been that the self created in the image of God can find no fuller expression, no richer fulfillment, than the will of God. Surrender to the will of God means the crucifixion of a false self, greed and gluttony, the desire for personal acclaim, and the lust for money. When these idols have been placed at the foot of the cross and their worshiper has been crucified, the crucified God can act with resurrection power. To be united to the will of God simultaneously fulfills the person and fulfills God's purpose. With this surrender the servant of God has no need to exercise power and control over brothers and sisters. The crucified person is free, free to be the unique person God had in mind, free to receive life as a gift, free to live the will of God in the concrete circumstances of life. This choice gives life ultimate significance.

It was Friday evening. Tom MacGreggor, already tired from a particularly busy week, had had to call an emergency meeting of the Building and Grounds Committee when the air-conditioning unit burned out. It had turned into a difficult session that ran long, and Tom, completely enervated, was late getting home. Margie, already in bed but not asleep, gave him a kiss as he crawled between the sheets. All Tom wanted was a good night's sleep. He didn't want to think about ministry, the church, or anything else.

But sleep didn't come, so Tom got up to watch a little television, hoping to relax his mind. Flipping through the channels, he settled on a movie adapted from Victor Hugo's great novel, *Les Misérables.* He vaguely remembered the story about the escaped galley slave who became a successful manufacturer in nineteenth-century France, but the details of the plot had faded from memory.

In the beginning Jean Valjean, the escaped galley slave and the main character in the movie, was making his way through the city seeking food. None could be found. He was turned away from door after door. Finally, someone suggested that he try the bishop's house. After a rap at the door he was warmly received, given food, and bedded down for the night. Before dawn this man, who in every way looked the part of a runaway, rose, packed the bishop's silver in a knapsack, and left.

The next scene has him standing helplessly in the bishop's dining room, having been apprehended by the police. "We found this man leaving town," they were saying, "and he has a knapsack filled with silver that bears your initials!"

The bishop's housekeeper casts "I told you so" glances at her employer while he listens patiently to the report. All the while Jean Valjean stands with head bowed like a condemned man before the hangman's noose. The police inquire if the bishop's silver is missing.

With a sudden move, the bishop goes to the mantel on which sit two silver candlesticks. He picks up the candlesticks and thrusts them into the hands of Jean Valjean with these words: "Jean, don't you remember, I gave you the candlesticks also?"

Jean looks up. He is bewildered by this show of grace, which saves his life and protects the integrity of the bishop.

The bishop speaks. "Remember, Jean, I have discovered that life is to give and not to get!"

By this time Tom was hooked by the story. The events of the past week, the talks by Delos Franke, the challenge to his ministry, Jesus' and Paul's examples of servanthood—all these kept his eyes open and glued to the television set as the plot unfolded.

The story continued as Jean Valjean left the bishop's house. On the road from the city in which he had been treated with grace he experienced a conversion. From this point the story skips a number of years. The galley slave has become a successful manufacturer who has changed his name to Monsieur Madeleine; Jean Valjean is still being hunted by Javert, a police inspector who wishes to prosecute him and send him back to the galleys.

Three different episodes gripped Tom with the power of servanthood. First, a woman rearing a child comes to Madeleine's office. She is his employee in the mill. He gives her what she needs to survive.

On another occasion, a man is trapped under a wagon. No one can move the collapsed wagon off his crushed body. Madeleine, with the upper-body strength acquired from his years of rowing, pulls off his coat, crawls into the mud, places his shoulder under the axle of the broken wagon, and lifts it off the injured man. Inspector Javert watches and thinks, Where did he get such strength? He looks like a man from the galley.

Finally, Madeleine exposes his real identity. He has heard that Jean Valjean is being tried; he will be condemned to the gallows or the guillotine if he is found guilty. What does Madeleine do? He attends the trial. There before the judge stands a man who looks exactly like the Jean Valjean of the opening scene. He is demented; none of his words make sense. What difference would the death of this man make? Beside him stand companions who served with Valjean in the galley. The courtroom is filled. Everyone's eyes are suddenly drawn to Madeleine, the successful manufacturer.

He strides down the aisle to the judge's bench. Before the bench he speaks. "This man is not Jean Valjean; he does not deserve to die." Courageously, he confesses, "I am Jean Valjean." The crowd is aghast.

Then he turns to his old partners in the ship's hole. "Do you remember . . . ?" and he reels off incident after incident they shared together. In no way could he have known these facts if he had not been in the galley with them. He has run the risk. He has owned his identity.

How extraordinary, Tom thought to himself, that a fictional story could dramatize so clearly what I've been thinking about all week, the servanthood of the minister of Jesus Christ.

The scene in the bishop's dining room and the narrative that unfolded have made Tom determined to discover in his own ministry what the priest of God said.

"I have discovered that life is to give and not to get."

Appendix

The Guided Reflections in this appendix have been written for the serious reader. Each one is composed of a series of exercises to help you, the minister, reflect on your experience of pastoral ministry. The reflections correspond to the themes of the respective chapters.

Simply reading this material, even if it presents a renewed vision, will have minimal effect. You must make an investment of time and thought in the enterprise. Whether the reflections are done on consecutive days does not matter; what matters is that they are done.

The first step is to make a firm commitment to yourself to keep a journal as you go through the following exercises. In it write your responses and reflections. As you keep at this approach, the journal will begin to connect, one part with another; it will also give new insights back to you.

If you have not kept a journal before, let me offer some helpful suggestions. Begin by acquiring a notebook that will be easy to handle and comfortable to use. Some prefer a looseleaf style; others like spiral or bound notebooks. I also strongly suggest writing in longhand, in ink, not pencil. Of course, you may type your notes or even use a computer if you prefer.

Be sure to date each entry by month, day, and year.

Self-discipline is important in journal keeping, so write regularly, but don't be discouraged if you can't write every day. Don't give up your commitment just because you miss a day or two.

Finally, bear in mind the difference between keeping a diary and keeping a journal. A diary simply records external events, occurrences, observations. A journal takes what is recorded and puts it into a larger context or imbues it with a deeper meaning.

Journal writing is a spiritual exercise. Perhaps as you write, you might think of yourself as making a confession of your ministerial life to God.

Guided Reflection 1

These exercises will guide you in a review of your call.

FIRST DAY: Make a list of the ways you have spent your time this past month. Identify the fragments of your life. Read them over. Get a feel for your life.

SECOND DAY: Identify the basic elements of your call. List the experiences that contributed to it; reflect on them; absorb energy from these memories.

THIRD DAY: What other elements can you add to the formation of your call?

FOURTH DAY: Read again the symptoms of the "loss of call" and "pastoral stagnation" in chapter 1. Which characteristics describe you? Reflect on your sense of call in light of these empty experiences.

FIFTH DAY: In an act of intentional surrender, accept yourself and your feelings of inadequacy and failure. Own your call from God and the life that is yours. Be present to your life today.

SIXTH DAY: Face squarely the issues of your life. In the way Martin Luther spoke of his baptism, say to yourself, "I have been called by God." In your consciousness, fuse your call with these issues. "I am this person with these issues, and I have been called by God!"

SEVENTH DAY: Review the week's reflections. Identify those aspects of your life for which you wish to give thanks to God.

Guided Reflection 2

These exercises will put you in contact with the forces in your spiritual matrix that shape your relation to God.

FIRST DAY: Think about the fact that you are. Try to picture the time before you were. Reflect on the time when you will be no longer. Feast on the fact of your being now. Write your feelings in your journal.

SECOND DAY: What is God like for you? Choose one attribute of God and think about it through the day.

THIRD DAY: What support for your spiritual life is offered you by members of Christ's body? Other persons? Nature? Family?

FOURTH DAY: What influences in the community affect your life? With whom do you have a relation outside the church membership? With whom should you relate? To what ministry does the community call you?

FIFTH DAY: Consider this time of your life. Review the reflections of the first day. Let yourself feel the depth, brevity, and urgency of your time now.

SIXTH DAY: Where is your call leading you? Toward what does your history in ministry point? What intuitions do you have about your future? What are your dreams and hopes? Your fears?

SEVENTH DAY: Review the six directives of this week. Think about each aspect slowly, consecutively, and receptively. Let your life come together in wholeness. Give thanks to God.

Guided Reflection 3

These exercises will make you aware of your capacities for a deepened relation with yourself and with God.

FIRST DAY: All four functions of consciousness enable you to relate to God. Complete the following sentences: "God is like . . . (intuition). As I review the history of my life, I see God in these events: . . . (sensation)."

SECOND DAY: "God's love has been manifest to me in that while I was a sinner Christ died for me." What does this statement mean? (thinking). How does this make you feel? (feeling).

THIRD DAY: Take a look at yourself. How do you inflate your ego? About what are you touchy or sensitive? Secretly, how do you wish people thought of you?

FOURTH DAY: You might get an indication of your shadow by answering these questions: If you were being interviewed for a new call, how would you seek to impress the committee? What aggressive, destructive thoughts do you have? What fantasies do you have of which you are ashamed?

FIFTH DAY: Encounter your depths. Quiet your body; relax; let images begin to flow. After a few minutes of relaxation, write the images that rise in your consciousness.

SIXTH DAY: Ponder the meaning of wholeness (individuation). Image wholeness in your own life. Picture yourself living toward these images. Think about these images in relation to your life now. Let yourself feel the inspiration of these images.

SEVENTH DAY: "I am wonderfully and fearfully made." Feel the awesomeness of your personhood in its wholeness. Offer your whole self to God with gratitude.

Guided Reflection 4

These exercises will guide you in the process of becoming conscious of God in your life journey.

FIRST DAY: Identify the marker events in your life. (A marker event is a turning point, an important decision, a move, a change, or the like.) Read over them slowly, thoughtfully, reflectively. Feel the flow of your life.

SECOND DAY: Think of the space between each marker event as a period in your life. For each period write a short paragraph by completing the sentence, "It was a time when . . ."

THIRD DAY: Meditate on each aspect of the period you described on the second day. Give thanks to God for these periods of your life.

FOURTH DAY: From your present vantage point ask of each period, "What was God doing in this period of my life?" Write the ideas that come to you.

FIFTH DAY: Review each of the crisis stages Erikson describes. Use these as lenses to look at your unfolding story. Where have you lacked a favorable ratio between the positive and negative elements in each stage? How has this affected your spiritual development? Listen to failed crises as to invitations.

SIXTH DAY: Reflect on the present chapter of your life. How are these eight issues of personal growth affecting you now? Note the crises before you as well as those behind you.

SEVENTH DAY: Keep in focus the call of God, which is central to your spirituality. What is God now calling you to do or be? What experiences in the present confirm your sense of call?

Guided Reflection 5

These exercises will help you examine your pastoral piety, adopt new approaches, and embrace a more consistent discipline.

FIRST DAY: Describe your reactions to the word "piety." Write your definition of piety. How important is your piety?

SECOND DAY: Review your devotional history. What major influences have shaped your present understanding of piety?

THIRD DAY: Identify the ways you have sought to deepen your awareness of God in the last month. What devotional practices have been most nourishing to you?

FOURTH DAY: List the ways a deepened devotion to God could strengthen you.

FIFTH DAY: Review the different forms of piety and identify the practices or emphases that seem crucial for your spiritual development. Following the model of Tom MacGreggor, define for yourself a comprehensive style of Christian spirituality.

SIXTH DAY: Read over yesterday's description of spirituality and edit it. Make definite commitments regarding time, place, and discipline for deepening your piety.

SEVENTH DAY: Begin your new discipline. Expunge guilt, failure, and inadequacy from your mind. God wills to meet you *now*, in new ways and with grace. Give thanks for new beginnings.

Guided Reflection 6

These meditation exercises will help you embrace the role of Christ-bearer.

Write an interpretive paraphrase of each of the following verses. For example, as a paraphrase of John 14:16–17: "Christ has asked the Father to give me another helper, one to take Christ's place; the Spirit of Truth was with us in the person of Jesus but now will be in me; the spirit of Christ lives in my consciousness."

FIRST DAY: "If a man loves me, he will keep my word, and my Father will love him, and we will come to him and make our home with him" (John 14:23). (These verses refer to all believers, but we are making application to the minister.)

SECOND DAY: "You did not choose me, but I chose you and appointed you that you should go and bear fruit and that your fruit should abide" (John 15:16).

THIRD DAY: "But when he who had set me apart before I was born, and had called me through his grace, was pleased to reveal his Son to me, in order that I might preach him among the Gentiles, I did not confer with flesh and blood, nor did I go up to Jerusalem to those who were apostles before me" (Gal. 1:15–16).

FOURTH DAY: "I have been crucified with Christ; it is no longer I who live, but Christ who lives in me; and the life I now live in the flesh I live by faith in the Son of God, who loved me and gave himself for me" (Gal. 2:20).

FIFTH DAY: "For as many of you as were baptized into Christ have put on Christ" (Gal. 3:27).

SIXTH DAY: "Here we are, then, speaking for Christ, as though God himself were making his appeal through us. We plead on Christ's behalf: let God change you from enemies into his friends!" (2 Cor. 5:20, TEV).

SEVENTH DAY: In three or four paragraphs define what it means for you as a minister of God to be a Christ-bearer.

Guided Reflection 7

The exercises in the first six reflections have been focused on the minister as spiritual person. The exercises in the final four reflections concentrate on doing spirituality in the pastoral roles.

FIRST DAY: Imagine time without any structure—no minutes, hours, days, years, periods. (Perhaps a meditation on Genesis 1:1–2 will help.) Write your reflections.

SECOND DAY: Write a short first-person paragraph describing your role in the structuring of time. Begin with the sentence, "I am an artisan of time who . . ."

THIRD DAY: Before you lead worship this week, image yourself as the bearer of Christ. Speak and act as one being directed by Christ. After the service write your reflections.

FOURTH DAY: Reflect on the great celebrations of the Christian year. How do these seminal events in Christ's life provide a structure for history? How do these events inform your role as an artisan?

FIFTH DAY: As you perform the routine pastoral functions, think of yourself as a bearer of Christ. What insights, obstacles, or inspiration does this identity offer you?

SIXTH DAY: Image the Lord's Supper as a time of cleansing the soul, nourishing the people, and orienting persons' lives. How can you make it an invitation to healing, reconciliation, and celebration?

SEVENTH DAY: What is your role in all these functions in forming the corporate spirituality of the congregation? Give thanks to God for the appointment you have as a minister.

Guided Reflection 8

These exercises will guide you in the initial steps of spiritual direction.

FIRST DAY: Imagine yourself in the role of a spiritual guide. What are your positive and negative feelings?

SECOND DAY: Figures 6 and 7 outline different stages in spiritual awareness and spiritual maturity, before and after formulating a personal faith. Use them as lenses through which you view another's story. (You may wish to adapt them to express more accurately your own theological commitments and your Christian experience.)

THIRD DAY: Review and evaluate Tom MacGreggor's agenda for offering spiritual guidance. Revise it for yourself.

FOURTH DAY: Name three persons you know who probably need help with their relation to God. Pray for them, seeking God's guidance in initiating a conversation with each about God in their lives.

FIFTH DAY: Interview one of these persons. Ask the person to share his or her faith story.

SIXTH DAY: Reflect on your offer and your experience of seeking to be a spiritual guide. What positive experiences did you have? What would you do differently next time?

SEVENTH DAY: Pray for guidance in finding a spiritual guide for your life. Give thanks to God for using you in ways that you do not know about.

Guided Reflection 9

These exercises will clarify your leadership role in the body of Christ.

FIRST DAY: Read 1 Corinthians 12:12–27. Picture your congregation as the body of Christ. Apply the Pauline images to specific persons.

SECOND DAY: If the earthly life of Jesus provided the model for the church's ministry, what should the church be doing? With what attitude?

THIRD DAY: Make a list of all the ministries of your church. How does each of these express the person of Christ? How could each more fully express his Spirit?

FOURTH DAY: Describe your vision for this church five years from today. What new ministries will it be doing? What present ministries will have ceased? What will be the nature of its fellowship?

FIFTH DAY: If you are the re-presentation of Christ, what changes do you need to make in the way you give leadership to the planning and guiding functions?

SIXTH DAY: With which group will you begin these changes in style? When? What risks do you feel in this change?

SEVENTH DAY: How will you train leaders to help you with this new vision? Name six persons with whom you will begin. Thank God for this role.

Guided Reflection 10

These exercises will assist you in identifying your role as a servant of Christ.

FIRST DAY: Read Philippians 2:5–11. What is the meaning of the phrase "mind of Christ"?

SECOND DAY: The stages of Christ's descent according to Paul are: (1) emptied himself, (2) took the form of a servant, (3) humbled himself, (4) became obedient unto death, (5) the death on a cross. What specific forms does this descent take in your ministry?

THIRD DAY: How does the theme of Christ's ministry—"I came not to be ministered unto but to minister"—inform your ministry?

FOURTH DAY: Name six persons in your context of ministry who need your servanthood. What resistance do you have to serving each? What is one concrete act of ministry you can offer each?

FIFTH DAY: With what person or body of persons do you have difficulty humbling yourself? What lies at the root of your resistance?

SIXTH DAY: Discuss the role of the pastor as a servant of the Lord with one leader in your congregation. How do you distinguish between servant of the Lord and servant of the people?

SEVENTH DAY: Write your list of resolutions regarding servanthood in your journal. Write a prayer for God's help.

Notes

CHAPTER 1: The Minister of God

1. Karl Barth, *The Doctrine of Reconciliation,* in *Church Dogmatics,* vol. IV, 3, II, trans. G. W. Bromiley, ed. G. W. Bromiley and T. F. Torrance (Edinburgh: T. & T. Clark, 1962), p. 481.

2. H. Richard Niebuhr, *The Purpose of the Church and Its Ministry* (New York: Harper & Row, 1956). I have adapted Niebuhr's thoughts on the elements of call for our purposes here.

3. James Dittes, *Minister on the Spot* (New York: Pilgrim Press, 1970).

4. Yves M. J. Congar, *I Believe in the Holy Spirit,* trans. David Smith, vol. 1 (New York: Seabury Press, 1983), p. 69.

5. Carlo Carretto, *Letters from the Desert* (Maryknoll, N.Y.: Orbis Books, 1972), p. xv.

6. Barth, *The Doctrine of Reconciliation,* p. 496.

7. Carretto, *Letters from the Desert,* p. xv.

CHAPTER 2: The Matrix of Pastoral Spirituality

1. This story was inspired by a story I read in Anthony de Mello's book *The Song of the Bird* (Garden City, N.Y.: Doubleday & Co., Image Books, 1982), p. 10.

2. Victor C. Pfitzner, *Paul and the Agon Motif* (Leiden: E. J. Brill, 1967), p. 79.

3. Urban T. Holmes III, *Spirituality for Ministry* (San Francisco: Harper & Row, 1982), p. 12.

4. For a full discussion see James Fowler's *Stages of Faith: The Psychology of Human Development and the Quest for Meaning* (San Francisco: Harper & Row, 1981).

5. John K. Ryan, trans., *The Confessions of St. Augustine* (Garden City, N.Y.: Doubleday & Co., Image Books, 1960), p. 48.

6. Inspired by a story in *The Song of the Bird,* p. 12.

CHAPTER 3: Self-Awareness in Pastoral Spirituality

1. Peter Shaffer, *Amadeus* (New York: Harper & Row, 1980), pp. 7–8.

2. Ibid., p. 19.

3. Ibid., p. 46.

4. Ibid., p. 47.

5. Ibid., p. 95.

6. John T. McNeill, ed., *Calvin: Institutes of the Christian Religion,* Library of Christian Classics, Vol. XX (Philadelphia: Westminster Press, 1960), pp. 35–36.

7. Walter Hilton, quoted in Urban T. Holmes III, *A History of Christian Spirituality* (New York: Seabury Press, 1981), pp. 79–80.

8. C. G. Jung, *Memories, Dreams, Reflections,* ed. Aniela Jaffe, trans. Richard and Clara Winston (New York: Random House, Vintage Books, 1965), p. 206.

9. I have elaborated this view in *To Will God's Will: Beginning the Journey* (Philadelphia: Westminster Press, 1987).

10. Wayne G. Rollins, *Jung and the Bible* (Atlanta: John Knox Press, 1983), p. 36.

11. Jung, *Memories, Dreams, Reflections,* p. 117.

12. Ibid., p. 127.

13. See *To Will God's Will* for guidance in reconstructing your life story.

14. In *The Confessions of St. Augustine* you will find the kind of theological reflection on one's life that I am recommending. In this work Augustine reviews his whole life from the standpoint of faith, writing his review as a confession to God.

CHAPTER 4: Pastoral Spirituality as Process

1. Erik Erikson's division of the life cycle into eight recognizable stages is found in chapter 7 of his book *Childhood and Society,* 2nd ed., rev. and enl. (New York: W. W. Norton & Co., 1963), pp. 247–274.

2. Erik Erikson, *Identity—Youth and Crisis* (New York: W. W. Norton & Co., 1968), p. 92.

3. The chart on psychosocial crises was developed for classroom use by my colleague at Columbia Seminary, Dr. Jasper N. Keith. I have adapted it for usage here.

CHAPTER 5: Toward a Pastoral Piety

1. Morton T. Kelsey, *Companions on the Inner Way* (New York: Crossroad Publishing Co., 1983), p. 119.

CHAPTER 6: The Pastor as a Christ-Bearer

1. *The Birth of the Living God* by Ana-Maria Rizzuto (Chicago: University of Chicago Press, 1979) provides the basis for this idea.

CHAPTER 7: The Pastor as Artisan of Time

1. John H. Westerhoff III, *Living the Faith Community* (Minneapolis: Winston Press, 1985), p. 31.

CHAPTER 8: The Pastor as Spiritual Guide

1. The May material is from Tilden H. Edwards, *Spiritual Friend* (New York: Paulist Press, 1980), p. 130. I recommend this book to persons interested in being a spiritual guide.

CHAPTER 9: The Spiritual Dimensions of Pastoral Leadership

1. The four styles of leadership were suggested in a lecture by Dr. Robert Ramey, professor of ministry at Columbia Seminary.